INSTINCT
FOR GRADUATES

Instinct

Reposition Yourself

Maximize the Moment

64 Lessons for a Life Without Limits

Making Great Decisions

The T.D. Jakes Relationship Bible

The Great Investment

The Ten Commandments of Working in a Hostile Environment

On the Seventh Day

Not Easily Broken

So You Call Yourself a Man?

Woman, Thou Art Loosed!

He-Motions

Mama Made the Difference

God's Leading Lady

Can You Stand to Be Blessed?

Let It Go: Forgive So You Can Be Forgiven

INSTINCT
FOR GRADUATES

The Power to Unleash Your Inborn Drive
and Face Your Unlimited Future

T.D. Jakes

FaithWords

New York   Boston   Nashville

Unless otherwise indicated, scripture quotations are taken from The Message. Copyright © 1993, 1994, 1995, 1996, 2000, 2001, 2002. Used by permission of NavPress Publishing Group. All rights reserved worldwide.

FaithWords
Hachette Book Group
1290 Avenue of the Americas
New York, NY 10104

www.faithwords.com

Printed in the United States of America

RRD-C

First Edition: April 2015
10 9 8 7 6 5 4 3 2 1

FaithWords is a division of Hachette Book Group, Inc.
The FaithWords name and logo are trademarks of Hachette Book Group, Inc.

The Hachette Speakers Bureau provides a wide range of authors for speaking events. To find out more, go to www.hachettespeakersbureau.com or call (866) 376-6591.

The publisher is not responsible for websites (or their content) that are not owned by the publisher.

Library of Congress Cataloging-in-Publication Data has been applied for.

ISBN 978-1-4555-3410-4 (hardcover) / ISBN 978-1-4555-3409-8 (ebook)

Contents

INTRODUCTION 7

1
Be You: The Instinct to Embrace
Your Uniqueness 11

2
The Ride of Your Life: The Instinct to Pursue
Your Dreams 23

3
Fuel for the Journey: The Instinct to Connect to
Faith and Community 35

4
The Job Hunt: The Instinct to Pursue
Your Career and Calling 47

5
Tour Guides: The Instinct to Find and
Treasure Mentors 63

6
Travel Mates: The Instinct to Make,
Keep and Change Friends 75

7

*The Home Front: The Instinct to Set Up
Your Home for Success 85*

8

*Farewell: The Instinct to Move from Dependent to
Independent Status 97*

9

*The Hunt for Love: The Instinct to
Find Life-long Love 107*

10

*The Travel Fund: The Instinct to Save, Spend,
and Increase 117*

11

*You've Got This: The Instinct to
Survive the Dark 129*

12

*The Call of the Wild: The Instinct to
Serve Freely 139*

13

*Enjoy the Ride: The Instinct to
Lighten Up 149*

14

*Lessons on the Journey: The Instinct to
Learn For Life 159*

15

Soar Eagle, Soar; The Instinct to Fly 167

Introduction

ONGRATULATIONS! You're holding this book *Instinct for Graduates* and that could mean only one of two things: you've just graduated, completed a program, checked off a to-do and accomplished a life-long dream *or* you know someone who has recently graduated and you're extremely proud and want to share this little tool to help your grad continue to soar and chase unlimited dreams. Either way, congratulations are in order. Completing something you've set out to do deserves to be celebrated—and supporting someone who has achieved a goal is just as important. It's no doubt an exciting time for you and those who have supported you, and I'm happy to journey along with you at such a pivotal time.

What an awesome place to be—standing at the crossroads of obtaining a goal—one you've no doubt worked hard to attain—and looking ahead to something new—college, graduate school, a new job, a new business, a new start in life. Exciting times are ahead.

And, if you're like me and everyone else I know, you're

probably experiencing a tinge of another emotion right now. Some may call it the fear of the unknown, the fear of change, or a touch of anxiety as you cross the street and begin anew. But, that's why I've written this book and other *Instinct* books. I believe wholeheartedly that God has already put exactly what you need inside of you to help you succeed. This thing called *instinct* is inside each of us—it is an inborn drive waiting to be unleashed. And when we tap into it and set it free, we gain the ability to add flair and confidence and knowledge to whatever we do. Tapping into our instinct allows each of us to bring the little extra "*something something*" that no one else has been wired to do quite like we do it. Connecting to our instinct can help us know when to move or which job to take or even who to choose as a lifelong partner. Instinct is important. And instinct is powerful.

So, I invite you to journey with me as I share some insights on *Instinct*—particularly for those of you standing in front of new opportunities. I see life as a journey and it reminds me of the new insights God gave me during a safari in South Africa. The safari was everything I had dreamed of and more. Right there on the tip of the continent, I got some new revelations on how to better live my life, run my businesses and share with God's people. On the trip of a life-time, I had a bird's eye view of God's amazing animal kingdom and how God has wired creation to work instinctively, and it changed the way I think and act.

I want to share these nuggets with you as you enter a new kingdom and claim new territory so that you can tap into your *instinct* and become all that God has designed you to be. It's a wild ride out there. I invite you to grab your bags and journey with me so we can discover what God has placed inside of you and unleash it to propel you into your unlimited future. I know you're ready for the challenge.

Let's go.

T. D. Jakes

1

Be You:
The Instinct to Embrace
Your Uniqueness

AS YOU FUEL UP FOR YOUR NEXT LEG OF THIS journey—taking a moment to celebrate your accomplishment and checking your GPS to see what's next—consider not only celebrating your graduation but also celebrating the person you are and the person you've become. In short, take the time to get to know who you are; decide to love the person you are; and embrace all that is you. Discover what makes you really tick. When you're busy accomplishing a goal and checking off a dream on the bucket list, you sometimes lose sight of who you are. So graduate, what better time to stop, reflect and get you together before you head off to your next destination. You're going to need to know who you are in order to fulfill your destiny and utilize your God-given instinct.

Starting a new chapter in life makes it more important than ever to unleash your true self and embrace what God has put inside of you—it's how you learn to live by instinct. Living instinctively means aligning our lives with the inner wisdom of who we really are and what we were made to do. In order to get in line with ourselves and ultimately our purpose, we've got to know who we are at our core. Our creator has equipped each of us with a fundamental instinct that draws us to our purpose. Knowing who you are is directly related to being able to recognize instinct and to follow it.

So right now, determine that you will take this bold and life-changing step, pick up some courage and figure out who you are—and then liberate yourself to be the wonderful and unique person you are.

Take a deep breath—and a little break—before you start up again and tackle that next goal. Assess yourself. Don't worry, this is not another test—you've had enough of those for now. This is really a moment to be with yourself and reflect on your uniqueness—what makes you you, what makes you come alive and feel invigorated, what gets you going. This course is all about you and your only task is to become a student of yourself. This just might be your toughest subject yet. Mastering this course requires attention and dedication, but the fruit it yields will put you on the course to succeed in life. The course of self-awareness is designed to put you in touch with that little inner voice called *instinct*.

Those successful people who are in tune with their inborn drive know that God, the master designer, has equipped all people with a fundamental instinct that draws us to our divine purpose. These people who are engaged with their life's calling and purpose rely on something that cannot be taught. The long classes and longer nights of studying don't teach you instinct. It's something inside that propels you to do what others cannot do like you do it—instinct followers naturally enhance what they touch in a way that others can't explain. This sense of potential being realized is more fulfilling than any paycheck. It is the true feeling of fitting in, like a piece in a puzzle, to form a greater picture than you could ever imagine. It is the innate satisfaction that comes when you give the gift—in just the way only you can do it— to the world. It's like giving the biggest, best Christmas gift to a loved one—you feel good! You feel satisfied! You feel joy—and who wouldn't want to live life with that feeling?

And knowing who you are and were fashioned to be is the start of being in touch with your instinct. It's the beginning of a life-long, joy-filled and satisfying journey. Once we embrace this instinct of identity, we understand why we are so shaped and designed. We realize why we were rejected in some places, why we grew bored by other roles, and why over and over we're haunted by the possibility that there's some place, some plan, some design to which we should be aligned. The most fulfilled, confident people live their lives in the very midst of instinct. These individuals have answered the question, moved into the sweet spot, and been guided by God whose design is revealed in them. They are in their zone—and everyone around them can tell. When we have the courage to leave the familiar and step into the destiny to which our instincts keep drawing us, we can live the same way. And it starts with truly being in touch with who we are, what we like, and how we are wired.

Sometimes our parents, our teachers, even our friends and our own minds can make us think we are not enough or are too much. They try to influence us to act a certain way or be a certain way rather than who we are. Not all of their attempts to make us fit in a certain box are ill-willed. They more than likely want the best for us and see things from their perspective. If you're going to be successful, you are going to need to relinquish what others want you to be and become who you know you truly are and are designed to be. This includes letting go of your own negative thoughts and attempts to fit in a place you don't belong. If you are a circle, you cannot fit into a square. Learn who you are as a circle. Embrace your shape as a circle, be the best circle you can be and live as a circle. You were created to be you. At this point in your journey, it's a great time to release the shackles from your mind and commit to living your own life. Embracing you and all that is you.

Think of it this way, you are the most fascinating person you will ever know so allow the true you to come out—whether that is the softer side, the edgier side, the creative side, the more organized side, the driven side, the liberated side, the who-cares-what-people think side, and the it-may-seem-crazy-to-you-side but this-makes-me-feel-alive side.

Getting to know you, the one created by God to be you and only you, is like gardening. An astute gardener always takes time to prepare the ground before planting seeds. The gardener tills the ground, which means the gardener gets the soil ready to hold the seeds. It's important to have good, nutrient rich soil before planting the seeds to guarantee the plants have the best chance of surviving and producing strong, healthy crops.

In your self-awareness 101 course on you and only you, *you* will begin to till the ground and get the soil ready. In the turning over of the soil and the memories of times where you felt your best and most alive, you will get your ground ready for harvesting. Having the healthiest soil means seeds have a better chance of growing into healthy plants and fruitful crops. Good soil helps the plants break through the ground to do what they were designed to do—flourish and provide nourishment. Your seeds have already been planted by God; tilling the ground will make the soil ready to produce the good fruit God has deposited. By tilling your ground, you can discover the seeds that God planted even in your mother's womb (Psalm 139:13) and by getting the soil ready, you will see the plants burst through the surface of your conscious and bear fruit—fruit that will flourish and nourish your soul. Your seeds are waiting to burst forward with the special, tasty, plump, juicy fruit that says: I'm living the life I am supposed to live. I'm following my dreams and I have an unlimited future.

You Were Born For This...

The story of Moses provides a good example of what happens when God uses your unique identity to connect you to your purpose so you can yield a bounty of fruit. Moses' seed was planted at his conception and as he grew and tended to his soil, God provided the rain and the right conditions to make his fruit flourish. Moses was born during a turbulent time for the Israelites. In fact he was hidden in a basket by his mother and rescued by an Egyptian princess; this Israelite child, who wasn't supposed to live, was taken and raised in the king's palace. But somehow, deep down inside, Moses knew he was an Israelite and he had a connection to his people—even though he was raised elsewhere. At the root, at the heart, he was an Israelite. And, he was a liberator of his people—well before he parted the Red Sea. Exodus 2 records him getting angry at an Egyptian who hit an Israelite—Moses became so mad that he killed the Egyptian. (Talk about passion!) Then Moses tried to stop two Israelites from fighting—again his passion was for these people and he wanted them to live in harmony. Fast forward, 40 years of living in the wilderness, running from the Egyptians and probably from his calling, Moses encounters the burning bush and makes up several excuses why he can't liberate the Israelites (Exodus 3). But God had chosen Moses way back at birth and had implanted a special connection and love for these people. So who better to go and tell Pharaoh to let God's people go than Moses?

And that's exactly what God has in store for you—a special assignment, a special calling to do something God has placed inside of you. God had something specific and uniquely for you when God formed you in your mother's womb. Find out who you are so you can find out what you were created for. Your calling is directly connected to your identity and your uniqueness. Your instincts can guide you to what you love but may not have allowed yourself to admit. Invest in what is already inside of you—you will be amazed by what comes out.

What are you passionate about? What do you love to hate? There are clues all around you, my friend. Use pictures to jog your memories of times when you were your happiest; what were you doing? Think about times when you felt accomplished and satisfied; what had you done? What triggered the fulfillment? What do you love but may not have allowed yourself to admit? Dredge up your favorite memories of childhood and what gave you pleasure (or what got your blood boiling). What would you perhaps kill for? (Now don't run out and do that, but what would make you so mad that you'd want to defend it with all of your might?) Know that whatever once had the power to float your boat can still rock your world. And it holds the key to unlock your combination to an unlimited future. Your passions and your uniqueness hold the distinct, personalized combination to connect you to your future.

Look at your past and see what it is telling you about you; there are clues in your history that will predict your destiny. Moses started off living authentically; standing up for what he thought was right. He didn't have it all planned out; he didn't even think he had all of the skills he needed—but he did have the inner drive, the inner desire to be true to himself and his people. His Red Sea moment was awaiting him.

When you are being you—living as God has created you— following the inclinations deep inside of you (yes, even the ones that may seem odd and out of place), God is equipping you and shaping you and preparing you for your destiny. Embrace it. Follow it. Love it. Learn from it. Allow God to use your passions. You want to be able to exclaim: "This is what I was born to do!" Being true to the person God created you to be can lead you to that point—to your Red Sea moment.

In the words of Steve Jobs, the famous founder of Apple who followed his instinct to produce products that have changed the world: "Have the courage to follow your heart and your intuition. They somehow already know what you truly want to become. Everything else is secondary."

Know who you are and have the courage to be that person—every day.

Wisdom for the Journey

Your creator knows you best; ask God to reveal who you are and celebrate!

Oh yes, you shaped me first inside, then out;
you formed me in my mother's womb.
I thank you, High God—you're breathtaking!
Body and soul, I am marvelously made!
I worship in adoration—what a creation!
You know me inside and out,
you know every bone in my body;
You know exactly how I was made, bit by bit,
how I was sculpted from nothing into something.
Like an open book, you watched me grow from conception to
birth;
all the stages of my life were spread out before you,
The days of my life all prepared
before I'd even lived one day.

Psalm 139:13-16, MSG

Be your best you—no one else can.

2

The Ride of Your Life:
The Instinct to Pursue
Your Dreams

OKAY GRADUATE, BUCKLE UP, ADJUST YOUR SEAT and secure the hatch, it's time to live the life you've been destined for. You've already accomplished one major goal and can say you have the diploma, degree, certificate, which is also your key to the next door awaiting you. You've embraced your uniqueness and understand better some of the distinctive characteristics and gifts that make you *you*—and you understand that they can lead you to your destiny.

But how do you get there? How do you attain the big goal you've determined as your future? How can a dream come true when you feel like you're at the starting line of a long, uncertain course?

I believe living according to your instinct is the key to realizing dreams, and in this chapter, we're going to look a bit deeper at how your instinct can help you connect the dots of your life and set you on the path to attaining those goals that make this life worth living. We have been blessed to live at such an exciting time as now. I want you to run this course with so much passion and purpose and fulfillment that when you get to the end of this race, you can say you've truly enjoyed the journey. You can look back and know that your running was done with a purpose. Your journey was filled with moments that screamed: "I'm living the life I am supposed to live." I want you to be able to glance back over your life when you get to the finish line and proclaim: "I've fought the good fight and I've done exactly what God placed me on this earth to do." Now, that sounds like a life well-lived.

Instinct can help you follow God's path for your life, which will no doubt be the most fulfilling path. Following your inner drive and inborn wisdom can keep you in line with God, your master planner and creator. Your inner wisdom can propel you forward—even along a path that is not well traveled. Instinct is what makes you go for the job no one else would ever consider—because you have an inclination that it is in the direction you're traveling or will give you the skills you need for tomorrow. (More on that job hunt in Chapter 4.) Instinct will show you how to excel while flipping fries at McDonald's, which will get the attention of the manager or better yet an influential customer who has a bigger, more meaningful job to offer you. Instinct will get you noticed and your work commended.

Because our instincts are the treasure map of our souls'

satisfaction, our inner being has a hunch of where we should go, how we should do it, and when we should do it. The key is discerning that hunch, trusting that hunch and working it for our benefit. Always keep the treasure map open and in sight when making decisions. Your instinctive and internal map is not like anyone else's; it is uniquely designed with you in mind. It includes your distinct experience, makeup, gifts and talents. Stay in touch with your map, it is the GPS of your life. When you misstep and your internal GPS tells you to recalculate and make a U-turn on this journey, do so as soon as possible. U-turns are allowed—just ask your navigation system. Study your map—who you are, what peaks your interest, what makes you raise your eyebrow—what is inside of you and screaming to come out. Consistently follow your inner drive and discover a life you could not only dream of, but could not even imagine in your wildest dreams. It's time to find the thing you were created to do, the people you were meant to affect, and the power that comes from alignment with your purpose.

Start by reminding yourself what makes you different and unique. What gifts and skills do you possess? Which ones are you actively investing in? Investing in your gifts and skills means you are working on sharpening them— through formal training, reading or intentional observation. You want to use your God-given gifts so you want them to be the best they can be. Sharpening gifts is an instinctive way of preparing the way to increase—to multiply your reach as well as what you may get in return for using your gifts. It's a smart thing to sharpen your gifts.

And it's just as wise to know which skills you have that need more sharpening or extra help? Yes, a basketball player may be skilled in a jump shot and have an innate gifting to make more baskets than not. But you better believe if that player is a star, he has put in lots of practice, watched tons of video, and listened to the best of the best coaches to sharpen that jump shot. And if you value the gifts and skills God has given you, you too will put in hours of practice time to perfect that gift. How do you plan to get your God-given skills in tip-top shape? Perhaps your full-time job should be one that sharpens your innate gifts and skills? Maybe it is your side gig or your hobby that enhances that set of skills. Whatever it is, invest in you so you can get the highest return on those skills.

Now you may have a skill that everyone else seems to possess, but don't down play your uniqueness. No one else has your story, no one else has endured exactly what you have endured, no one else has been in the same set of circumstances, with the same resources, with the same perspective as you. What you bring to your gifts and skills can only be brought by you—so don't be shy, go ahead and do you—as only you can do it.

When you begin developing your skills, look for more and more opportunities to utilize them—to help others as well as yourself. Be free, be generous, be wise as you select opportunities to share your investment. Look for those clues and those times when you feel most alive and most happy—this is a direct correlation to the path you are supposed to be on. I'm not talking about the mere emotion of happiness, I'm talking about when you get excited. It could be a challenge—you know instincts like to be challenged. They like to have a little scare and a little rush. Pay attention to those moments so you'll know where your compass lies and can be better lead on this journey.

As you listen to your GPS, don't be afraid to roam beyond your present coverage. It's not time to play it safe. Yes, wisdom is encouraged, but safety can be overrated. Venture outside of your comfortable places. Move away from your neighborhood—if only for a day. You might find some people living quite differently than you are—and you might like it. Seeing new things, learning new ways of doing and being can awaken your senses and raise the magnitude of your dreams. A new vision of where you'd like to be can be the impetus to activate those instincts to put your gifts and talents to use. Roam beyond your present coverage. Roaming charges are free on the instinct plan—and they can yield some great benefits.

You've Got A Lot To Gain

Our instincts provide the key to unlocking our most productive, most satisfying, most joyful lives, which in turn allows us to have the rides of our lives. At the heart of our instincts we discover our primary purpose, which provides the message or mission by which we live out our gifts and talent. Yes, your mind may guide you in what to do, but the heart affirms your passion to do it. Your heart moves you to motion and gives you the clues to finding deeper passion and fulfillment. It's how you were wired. It's how I was wired. Know that nothing we have created can replace how we've been created. God has instilled in each of us a passion that ignites when we are operating in our true gifting and calling.

Instinct is not about being the smartest, but it is about being in tune with your inner drive and it answers the question what are you good for—what is your purpose. And when you're following that inner drive, you have the key to living a fulfilled life.

Living by instincts naturally enhances everything and everyone around you. And success will naturally come. Aligning your intellect (what you know from the books, training, experience) with your instincts (what you just know because of who you are) produces the fruits of your labors that are plump and juicy—and that everyone wants to taste and enjoy.

Don't get it twisted, living this type of life is not easy. It requires hard work and dedication, but let me tell you, the internal satisfaction will fuel your desire to accomplish even larger dreams. Pursue your passions and you will discover the fulfillment that comes from living by instinct.

Think about how your uniqueness is connected to your passions and purpose. Try not to limit your thinking. Allow yourself to describe all of the things you can do to fulfill these passions and purpose. And don't just think about a job. There is a difference between a job and a career and a calling (and we have more on that later).

Think about David (1 Samuel 16). He was a "lowly" shepherd boy. Scripture says he took that calling and purpose seriously. He protected the sheep from bears and lions. He wasn't afraid of them; he did what he was naturally called to do. I can imagine David's heart for people and taking care of them and leading them was developed right there in the fields of Bethlehem when he was a mere boy, overlooked by his daddy. He was the youngest in a line of brothers who stood out, but that didn't stop David from doing his best and developing his skills and gifts—even if it was a thankless and forgotten position. We know David didn't remain a lowly shepherd boy; he was eventually promoted to King over Israel and he became the most infamous king in biblical history and the writer of many of the psalms we still quote to this day. How's that for a fulfilling life? What would have happened if David had been a lackluster shepherd? If he had thought: "I've got bigger dreams than this. I want to be King. I want to be famous. I want to slay that silly Philistine Giant and have people sing songs about me." Would his skills been developed? Would he have been brave enough to slay Goliath? Would his faith in God have been developed to the point that he was known as a man after God's own heart? Would his psalms have been so powerful that they still move us today?

David, even as a young shepherd boy, focused on doing the very best with what he was called to do. He practiced leading people and killing giants in the lowly fields of Bethlehem where he was called to be a shepherd boy.

Watch out for what you do now. Your life may not seem thrilling, but if you tap into your passion and do it with all you have, to the best of your natural ability, you will see how your purpose will form out of that, which is uniquely yours. You will see how God can blow your mind and fulfill your dreams. And like David, don't forget to thank him and to glorify him with your gifts. You've got some sheep to take care of, shepherd girl and shepherd boy.

Do what you are doing with all of your guts, tap into your core and follow your instinct. It will lead you on the ride of your life. Buckle up!

Wisdom for the Journey

God can do anything, you know—far more than you could ever imagine or guess or request in your wildest dreams!

Ephesians 3:20, MSG

Take delight in the Lord,
and [God] will give you your heart's desires.

Psalm 37:4, NLT

Do your best. Work from the heart for your real Master, for God, confident that you'll get paid in full when you come into your inheritance.

Colossians 3:23, MSG

Live life to the fullest, give it all you've got.

3

*Fuel for the Journey:
The Instinct to Connect to
Faith and Community*

NOW LET'S GET DOWN TO BUSINESS HERE. YOU want to be a success; you want to live passionately and enjoy this ride of your life; you want to embrace the *you* God created and walk in your uniqueness. That's awesome, and I applaud that (I encourage it!) At the core of the issue, it's about your connection to God and to others. You are meant to run on fully-charged batteries. Not the Duracell or energizer bunny type of batteries; your power comes from God and from within. If you don't have a connection to your power source, your batteries run dead. You are ineffective and basically useless. Ever tried to talk or surf the net on your phone with a low battery? It gives you a little juice but soon warns you that you need to connect your charger to get more power. No one has created a gadget that runs without electricity or some source of power. You too need power and recharging. Your battery is only able to do its job well if it is charged and ready to go when you flick the switch to turn it on. Get me?

Your recharging won't be found in a wall socket, but it can be found by connecting to your creator and manufacturer, and repeating. You constantly need a supercharge, power to guide you along this journey. How will you know how to get to your destination if you don't have a little light on the path? And who better to connect to for light than the source of light and life?

Well, let me put it this way. If you, instinct follower, dream catcher, achieving friend are expecting to live out your purpose and be ready for the job, you've got to have your batteries charged. A dead soul, a dead cell won't cut it. And those batteries need to be charged to go the long haul.

I think of the Christian journey as being connected to the power source. I think of Bible study and prayer as ways to charge your battery, your center, your cells. If you are connected to your power source, you are ready and charged—regardless of how dark it gets. When the lights go out, you can flick the switch and still do your job.

When you get discouraged, you can flip the switch and allow your spirit to remind you of who you are and who created you and what you were created for.

When a bump in the road causes the lights to go out (more on this in Chapter 11), you don't have to fret and panic and worry and throw in the towel. You can flick on your switch and allow your power source to still function.

Electricity—or alternative sources of power—can be useful, but you can't count on it all the time. Alternative sources are like momentum; they can take you to a certain point, but soon they will run out.

People rely on drugs, other people, material things, physical appearances to get them through, to give them what they need. But those things are alternative sources of power. They all run out of power and help—oftentimes much sooner than we expect them to. You need something everlasting and ever-ready if you're going to walk successfully through this trek, if you're going to be on this journey for the long haul. Your batteries have got to stay charged.

So how do you stay connected to the Truth, the Power-giver? In a world filled with meetings and busy dates, getting up for church on a Sunday morning is often an option we skip. Late nights on Saturdays make Sundays hard. But lucky for your generation, there are many other options other than all-day church on Sunday (ask your folks or grandparents about going all day and back on Sunday nights). I know churches that have Saturday services and mid-week services in downtown areas—especially for the busy professional. Many churches offer online services or live video streaming to services and Bible studies. You can get some Word in you whenever you need to. You can google a subject or pastor, you can go to You Tube and hear sermons (including mine), you can stream live, you can read books. You can even read the Bible on your phone. Come on, your generation should have power that no other has had—after all, you're always connected to something. Make that connection fruitful and connect to God—you've got access at your fingertips. Tap into it and keep those batteries charged.

Finding the right church may also mean forgoing some of the traditions you were raised thinking you should have. Now is the time to evaluate if you are doing something for tradition sake or because you truly believe it. Nothing is wrong with traditions—usually. But, they don't have to be followed just to be followed. If a tradition isn't working for you (and it is not necessarily biblical or important to you, like what day you worship on or your attire for church), let that tradition go. Look for a church that fits your personality. If you like praise and worship, it's a good idea to go to a church with a great music department. You want to make sure that church's theology is sound and in line with your beliefs too, but it's okay to look for good music if that is what will get you to return to the church and continue to get your batteries charged. If you are more of the silent worshipper, a more contemplative, meditative service might fit you. There's no shoe that will fit every foot. One size doesn't fit all when it comes to choosing a church. Explore, keep looking, talk to friends and co-workers. Finding a good church can take as much effort and dedication as finding the right job—and some may argue that it could be more meaningful.

When your core is taken care of, you have more strength. You can move better. You have less pains in other areas of your body. The same is true with your soul. When you've gotten that taken care of—have a great church—you will find other areas of your life changing. You'll have more strength to go through the dark nights; you'll have a better perspective to handle the rest of the week. Your mind will get renewed constantly when you have your core in place. Our minds are programmable; and what we put into them will directly reflect how we act. Your thinking and your attitude will determine your altitude.

Don't sleep on your center, your core. It may feel like you're catching up on sleep when you neglect regular church attendances, Bible study or prayer, but you're actually losing ground and neglecting the right programs to enter in your data base of a mind.

You also get charged by connecting with like-minded believers—that's why sitting in your bed watching on a computer isn't always sufficient. Schedule a Bible study and prayer group—get some power by rubbing elbows with believers. They might have a testimony or a smile or a hand shake that makes your day, gives you the reminder that you can go on. A church with a dynamic single's ministry might help you connect to like-minded people; a group with a powerful marriage ministry could help you and your spouse; a great kid's ministry could make your kids excited about learning of God; a church that needs your help as a teacher, musician, usher, administrator is only a few feet away from you—trust me.

There's something very powerful about participating in the ministry of a church or parachurch group. Whether you are building a house for a needy family with Habitat for Humanity, collecting school supplies for needy children, or teaching a Sunday school class, your problems and issues become less when you open up and give of yourself; helping others switches the focus from your issues to someone else's—even if for a moment. And that's called perspective. So when your focus shifts to someone else—even for one hour of a week—you get to put your life in perspective. You may not have the dream job yet, but you have food. You may not feel like you're at the top of your game yet, but that sweet hug from a dirty little kid can make you feel like you're on top of the world. And that act of service, my friend, also connects you to your power source.

I look at attending church as getting fuel for your car; before a long trip, you always make a stop at the gas station. You know you need gas to make it to your destination. Some of us even go for the oil change and tune up to prepare for the journey ahead. Life is that journey and stopping by the prayer room and the sanctuary gives you that fuel to keep on going. When we are in constant contact with God, we are acknowledging that we can't do this trip alone. We need God by our side guiding us. We need an encounter with our creator to get directions for the next leg—the next moment. And even when our flesh (our bodies, our minds) don't want to come—they do get tired and Sunday is sometimes our only time off— our spirit reminds us that we need a charge. We need to stop by the gas station and get some fuel for the next week. Who knows what that week will hold? Who knows what strength you will need? Store it up, stash it away, hide it in your heart so it will be ready to be activated to ignite exactly what you need to keep pressing on and moving toward your future.

Getting to the gas station reminds me of a parable in the New Testament. The parable breaks down a message using illustrations the people of the time would understand. Just like I used fuel as a metaphor for power and being connected to God, Jesus used the story of the ten virgins to remind us to stay prepared and connected. The entire story can be found in Matthew 25:1-13.

The story is quite simple, yet its message is still powerful and applicable many centuries later. The ten women were going to meet a groom. They all carried lamps so they could see even when it got dark. However, five of those women brought extra oil so they could keep their lamps going—even when the oil inside went out; they would be able to use their extra oil when the current oil ran out. They had back-up oil. But, there were also five other women—the Bible calls them silly, foolish. These five women did not think to bring any extra oil. They apparently thought they could make it through the night with what they had in their lamps. Well, the groom didn't come as quickly as they thought and they did begin to run out of oil. They asked the five wise women to share and they said "no, go buy some more oil." And yes, you guessed it, when those five silly women went out to buy some more oil, the groom came and happily welcomed the five women to the wedding feast. The ones who were prepared made it to the wedding; they got what they came for. But when the five silly women finally found some oil and came back, they were not allowed into the ceremony. They missed their opportunity because they didn't have enough oil.

Life can get hard; your goals can seem far away. Stuff can happen to drain you of all the energy you have right now, of all the momentum you can start off with. Don't be like the silly women—stay prepared, stay fueled up.

Don't try to run this race with what you have now. It's not enough. Be sure to have a connection to your power source so you can get fuel when you need it. When you are weak, you can get rest. When you are tired, you can get help (Matthew 11:28). When you don't know where to go, you can get the guidance and assurance you need. God wants to give you that power and energy—you've just got to ask and be ready to receive it. Be ready for your encounter.

Daily scriptures on your smart phone, a devotional to read on the train, singing a song while getting dressed in the morning are also other powerful tools that help you keep your batteries charged and your eyes fixed on the power source, not yourself. This journey is not always easy going; you need to be ready and charged and connected to the One who is greater than you are.

Take a look at your calendar. When will you get your batteries charged? Make it a regular date. I promise you'll see more power with more prayer; you'll have more peace when you've communed with the Prince of Peace; you'll be recharged when you've given a little bit to someone else.

It's time to recharge and fuel up—it's going to be a long, wild journey.

Words for the Journey

"Are you tired? Worn out? Burned out on religion? Come to me. Get away with me and you'll recover your life. I'll show you how to take a real rest. Walk with me and work with me—watch how I do it. Learn the unforced rhythms of grace. I won't lay anything heavy or ill-fitting on you. Keep company with me and you'll learn to live freely and lightly.

Matthew 11:28-30, MSG

So let's do it—full of belief, confident that we're present-able inside and out. Let's keep a firm grip on the promises that keep us going. He always keeps his word. Let's see how inventive we can be in encouraging love and helping out, not avoiding worshiping together as some do but spurring each other on, especially as we see the big Day approaching.

Hebrews 10:22-25, MSG

4

The Job Hunt:
The Instinct to Pursue
Your Career and Calling

Y̲OU'VE ALREADY DISCOVERED THAT GOD HAS uniquely created you for a reason, and it's your responsibility to discover what that is and to do it like only you can do it. We often times think this is a job. We live in a society that honors titles and asks: "what do you do?" at every party you attend. And that way of thinking can get tricky. Oftentimes our jobs are not our callings; they are just jobs. They pay the bills, hopefully.

But what happens when your job is your calling? When you wake up in the morning excited about getting a task done because you know you have the tools and the passion and the experience to get it done in a unique way. That sounds like the sweet spot.

So how do you get to the leg of the journey where your calling is your job and you can wake up each morning excited to do it? Rarely do you wake up at a young age and open up the doors to your calling and feel like you're operating in it right then. Some lucky folks just might, but most of us build up to that, we work toward it and learn as we go, which is where I bet you are. And don't get me wrong, you can definitely have fulfillment in the entry place—you should—but look at it as stepping stones leading to your ultimate goal.

So, your first job or your early jobs can be indicators of what you are called to do. You can learn a lot sitting at the feet of someone else (ask the disciples!). If you are the low man or woman on the org chart in the company you work for, use this as an opportunity to gather lots and lots of information. And I'm not just talking about files and emails. Your workplace can be your laboratory for studying—while you get paid. What management practices inspire co-workers? What styles make them recoil and do less work? Who gets in early? Who stays late? Who's the person everyone goes to for answers? Whose presence is missed when they are on vacation or out of the office? Whose presence is celebrated when they are gone? Oh, yea, there's plenty to learn from those labs—without asking one question. And when you do have the opportunity to ask questions, find out how each person got to this path; how are they planning to get to the next one? Do they have some advice for you? (more on mentors, or tour guides, in Chapter 5.) Ask away. Most people love talking about themselves, and you'll be giving them permission to talk.

Your first job or early job can hold immeasurable treasures for you—if you have the perspective to learn all you can and to always keep moving forward. I know many people who've ended up in roles, careers, industries, and occupations that they never imagined. They didn't start out looking to go into their field; but they continued to stumble forward, taking advantage of each opportunity as it came. They found open doors and they kept walking forward through them. Their instincts guided them and helped them succeed.

And if you're at the crossroads between finishing a degree or program and looking for a job, take heart. We've all had to start somewhere. And many of us have had to restart over and over again. The reality is you need a job or a source of income. Determine if you have enough money to wait until you find the job you really want or if you may need to consider taking a job "in the mean-time—" one to help you pay your bills as you continue to search for one that matches your skills and training. And don't forget, the job we often think we *want* may not be the one we *need* right now. An assistant can learn a whole lot more on the support staff than on the team. Sometimes starting in a position that is less desirable to us can give us a view we would not get anywhere else. So, look in your area of interest, think about the places you'd like to work, but don't let them limit your search. Your need for a job can birth creativity and a new perspective.

I know people who would have never considered their current field if they didn't need a job desperately. And once they got on that job, they worked hard, observed carefully and learned a lot. Some got to do other functions in that company; others used that starting job to help them leap into other areas.

Not one size fits all—and that is true with jobs too. There are plenty of jobs you can do well, some you'll thrive at and others can point you toward your calling (and maybe let you know what you don't want to be doing or are not called to do). The hunting time is a great time to explore jobs and opportunities you may not have considered before. Dive into something different or new or something you've just never thought about. It's a wild jungle out there and you just might be surprised by where you find your true passions and abilities can line up and produce your calling and career. Can you relocate to another area, city or state? Or do you have reasons to stay put? Know the answers to these questions and let your searches reflect your answer. Do you need more training to get to a place you desire? How do you plan to get that training? Many jobs offer tuition reimbursement or training—and while you might not be ready to jump into school right away, it is important to look down the road as you consider your next move.

There are jobs out there. And the one you get today

doesn't have to be your only, life-long job. But, how you do that job—the attitude you take into it, the energy and effort you put into it—can set you on a course for fulfillment. How so, you ask? Think of it this way: on that job, you'll get training and have the same information as the next person doing that job. You can file the papers, send the email, answer the phone—just like that next person. But, if you're living by instinct, you can do it with the uniqueness only you have. Now I know it sounds pretty mundane and like it doesn't require any extra skills to do some of those tasks, but what if you brought your personality to that job? What if your optimism made you a pleasure to be around and made the boss invite you to lunch or made one of her clients notice you and ask if you were interested in helping on another project? What if the way you answered the phone—with a special oomph (not with a mundane, this-is-just-my job voice) and made someone's day seem just a bit brighter? Now you might not get a promotion for that, but you could be helping someone just by adding *you* to the mundane job. Do you get what I'm saying? Jobs can be routine. Tasks can be mundane, but you, my friend, are not. Bring *you* to every job you do and others will be blessed—and so will you.

Just meeting the demand, the job description, will never bring exceptional results. Exceed what is expected and do more than what is commanded. Veer into the creative that is within you and watch things flourish. Be on the lookout for an opportunity to add a little more than what is expected. Is there more you can volunteer to help out with on your own time? Why not get on a committee to plan the next social event; you might learn something valuable during one of those meetings or functions. If you know how to decorate, why not offer to come in an hour early and set up for the next function or holiday. You could get noticed for your commitment and your style.

You may not see the payday from your efforts right away or your impact immediately, but trust me, one day you will be able to look back and see how that first job, that "little" job prepared you for a career and a calling. And your efforts can make the difference in getting you noticed for the next position or next job that just might be your calling.

There are also some basic preparation tools that can help you on the hunt for your career and calling. Professional help with resume writing can make sure your resume represents you well: include your education, jobs, volunteer activities, etc. Social networks are your resume too, and not just the ones with job postings. Everything you write on the world wide web is just that—worldwide. What you post on Instagram and comment about on Facebook shows who you are—just make sure you're showing the world your best side. And it won't hurt to double check your spelling and grammar—it represents you.

Tell everyone you know that you are in the job market. Let them know your interests, but also listen to hear what they know about. It could be a job, company or field you haven't thought about. If a company is hiring, you want to know about it. And even if the company of interest is not hiring, consider informational interviews, shadow days and/or non-paid internships. Any time you can get in the door of a company, you can get information and access—which are critical in the hunt for a career. I've known people to get jobs in the oddest places—talking to someone on a train, bus or plane, requesting prayer at mid-week service, through a temporary agency job that turned permanent, showing up at just the right time when help was needed. Take a risk, go for it. You don't know what lies behind the closed door.

On the hunt, stay encouraged. Do whatever it is you will need to do to keep your spirit lifted and encouraged—even when the hunt is hard and a job seems far away. You want to present yourself as a positive, hardworking person, not as a downcast, hopeless one. The way you are feeling will be the vibe you give off. So think like a person who has a successful career and job—and you will give off the vibe that you are the person for the job. Invest in some nice interview clothes (shop at bargain and discount places if you are on a tight budget or use some of the money from your graduation gifts to invest in nice business attire that fits you well). No one ever got knocked out of the running because they showed up in a freshly pressed business suit. It never goes out of style. Everyone at the company may be dressed down, but you will look like you showed up for business. You can dress down when you get the job (if that is the lay of the land). Clean nails and groomed hair can go a long way to making a good impression too. These seemingly minor things won't get you the job, but they can count you out if neglected.

Once you've landed the big catch or found that job, there are some key things a true instinct follower will do:

Observe

Go in with the binoculars and magnifying glass. Remember you are an observer showing up for work in your laboratory. And you're not just looking for clues to your passions and calling, you are looking for the written and unwritten rules in your new environment. You are the new kid on the block—so act like it. Watch and listen to everything. Know who is who; who is the go-to person.

Be Kind to Everyone

And don't ever overlook the support staff. I don't care

what role you play in the company, make sure you treat everyone well—and that includes the person emptying the trash. Let me tell you, they know much more than you will ever suspect—the person who cleans up the mess often is privy to information others ignore. Simply speaking to the cleaning person may help you out down the road—not that that's the only reason you will be nice to him or her!

Be a Problem Solver

I often tell my staff: If you are not participating in finding the solution, you are a part of the problem. Everyone wants people who are helping find solutions. Don't just complain or talk about the problems, stretch your mind and help think of solutions—whether they are incorporated or not, at least you're thinking of ways to help instead of adding fuel to the problem fire.

Know Why

Don't be a pest, but find out why things are done. Don't just type in the information. Think about, listen for, ask why it is done. Leadership guru John Maxell says: those who know how to do a thing will always have a job, but those who understand why they did it will always be the boss. Look for whys!

Activate Instinct

The difference between knowing all about an animal and knowing where to find one is instinct. I can train you to do a job all day long, it's up to you to activate your instinct and add the unique ability only you can bring to the gig.

Keep Doors Open

Even as you exit your job—ready for the next move—be careful to always leave the door open. Whether you ever come back to this company or not, you may need a recommendation, a partner, networking opportunities. Some people relish the day they get to tell their boss to take this job and "shove it." But I never recommend that approach—regardless of how you feel. You just don't know where life will lead you and when your paths will need to cross again. Be known for how well you did your job, not for how you exited the company.

Do Your Best

No one should have to command you to do your best. And when you do your best—even at work—you do your best in life. Being fulfilled and working hard bubbles over into other areas of your life. You can't be a slouch at work and expect to come home and handle 50 tasks. You won't.

When talking about doing your best, I can't help but

think of Joseph's story. It's a long journey toward his destiny, but one well worth the read. You can find it in Genesis chapters 37, 39-50. Let me give you the cliff notes now. Joseph knew he was destined for greatness even at a young age—in fact he had dreams that his brothers would bow to him. And while he probably shouldn't have shared those dreams with his brothers at that time, he still held on to his dreams. And let me tell you, Joseph did not see the fulfillment of those dreams for quite a while. In fact, it would appear that his life went in the opposite direction of his vision. Instead of having his brothers bow down to him, Joseph was sold to foreigners. His dad thought he was dead. Joseph could have given up right then and decided his life was over and his dreams dead, but he still did his best work wherever he landed. Even in the foreign land of Egypt, he was promoted in his master's home and was put in charge of his house. Perhaps, an ordinary Joe would think he had arrived by being in charge and sat back and enjoyed, but Joseph stayed true to himself and to his God. He did what was right—even when given the golden opportunity to do wrong (check out his running, not walking, away from temptation in Genesis 39!) But doing right doesn't always lead to instant rewards. In fact when Joseph turned down the explicit offers from his boss's wife (yep, it's in the Bible), Joseph was punished. His honorable actions did not yield a payoff right away, but Joseph kept doing his best—even in jail. He was gifted with interpreting dreams and he used that skill and gift wherever he was. And when he thought folks would remember him, they didn't. But Joseph didn't give up when he could have. And one day, by God's divine timing, his cellmates remembered Joseph's gift and he was able to help save a nation. But not only did Joseph's hard work and gift from God save the foreign Egyptian nation, Joseph was able to save his father and his brothers—the same ones he had dreamed about long ago. His dream was now a reality. His brothers eventually bowed to him. His journey no doubt was probably not what he had in mind when he was a young boy, but the rough times, the servant status, nor the inmate position deterred Joseph from using his gift and doing right.

What is your gift? How can you use it wherever you find yourself—at the top of the chain, in the king's palace, in the jail cell or on the plantation of a job? Be like Joseph and don't allow your environment to dictate how you act. Live your life activating each and every gift God has placed in you—and your dreams will come true too.

Look for your Joseph moments today.

Wisdom for the Journey
Always do your best work!

Joseph replied, "Don't be afraid. Do I act for God? Don't you see, you planned evil against me but God used those same plans for my good, as you see all around you right now—life for many people…"

Genesis 50: 20, MSG

5

Tour Guides: The Instinct to Find and Treasure Mentors

TRAVELING ALONE ON THIS JOURNEY CAN BE
frightful, and it is downright impossible to operate as an island and truly be successful. Living our
purpose and finding fulfillment is directly related to how
we share with others. We share this journey with friends
and mates and of course God, but there are also people I
like to think of as tour guides who can make this journey
a little more pleasant and helpful.

Think of the role of a tour guide. They give tourists
immeasurable amounts of information about the locale;
they tell us what to pack, when to take pictures, what to
look out for. They guide us along this journey with helpful information—and a smile.

On the journey of life, mentors serve as tour guides.
They can point you in the right direction, share good
stories with powerful wisdom, remind you which places
are not safe and show you the hidden gems only "locals"
know about. Your mentors can be invaluable and make
this journey more meaningful.

Think of your school advisors, teachers, bosses, mentors and others who are in a position or place in life you'd like to get to. They may have a healthy relationship with themselves and God, they may have broken out and started their own thriving business, they may be great leaders in an organization—these are people who can help you navigate through this life and impart some welcomed wisdom. Our tour guides can see things from a different perspective—perhaps they sit in a different position with a different view. Perhaps they've already gone through some of the stuff we are dealing with and they can share insight. There is value in a multitude of wise advisors; they can help you succeed (Proverbs 15:22).

When considering advice from your multitude of advisors, it's a good idea to keep in mind which perspective your tour guide is coming from. There's a story about four blind men who touched an elephant and each of them described it differently, not knowing just how vast and multi-faceted an elephant is. One blind man touched the elephant's ears and said: "This beast is flat and flexible like a palm leaf." The other man grabbed the leg of the elephant and proclaimed: "No, this animal is sturdy and round like a tree trunk." The third man, who touched the elephant's tail, said: "Nope, you're both wrong; this creature is thin and wiry like a snake." The fourth blind man touched the side of the elephant and said: "Nope, you are all wrong. This animal is strong and sturdy like a stone wall." Yet, another man could have touched the ivory tusks and proclaimed something different. But the point of this story is that each person described what they observed. They didn't see the entire picture of the animal, which has multiple dimensions, different surfaces and sides. That's the story of life. One mentor can help you see one side of the story, another may guide you along a different path because they have a different view. None are wrong, in fact all know what they know because of what they are touching. So, you can gain valuable information from a multitude of counsel, but always know what side they are coming from. And in the end, you will have to use the information from your tour guides and your instinct to know which direction you need to go in.

Tour guides like to help and show you the way, that's what they've signed up for. But they also like to feel valued. No one wants you calling only when you need something. Consider developing relationships with your mentors that serve them well too. What can you do to help them? Perhaps help them out in a way they need too. They'll appreciate you and may impart even more information to you. Send thank you notes—a long forgotten gem in this world. Even if it is an email that says thanks, it is a reminder that you are grateful for their information. Some like to get an update on your life—let them know when you have a new job, receive an award, have a fun story to share. They want to know you're enjoying this ride of life and how they've impacted you.

Learning to receive feedback from others can be challenging—it does open us up and requires vulnerability. I think this is why developing a trusted relationship with mentors is important. You want to know that the attitude and the intention of the person providing feedback is helpful and has your best interest in mind. You have a lot to learn from feedback—it can help you improve in weak areas and overcome liabilities that may drag you down; feedback can also encourage you and point out strong areas you may have overlooked and not considered as strong. So knowing the intention and motives of the people providing you feedback is key.

Diversity in networks also makes great sense. Think of the word "net" and what it actually does. A net can catch a boat load of fish (ask Jesus' disciples), but nets are really just knots that are tied together and stretch out in different directions. If all those strings went in the same direction, you wouldn't have a net. When they reach out to different parts of the country, world, universe, you have a wider net that's available to catch even more fish. And that can help you fulfill your destiny and purpose in life. I think of a network as a variety of complementary talents and abilities working in harmony to achieve results beyond what you could achieve by sheer talent or hard work alone. It's better than operating in a silo. Reach out and develop a wide network—it will serve you well.

Networks provide exposure, a much needed ingredient when following your instinct and remaining in touch with your inborn drive. Exposure lets you see things you didn't know about or didn't consider. Exposure gives you a taste of something different, You may not like it—and then you never have to do it again or eat it again—but at least you've been exposed and have an informed opinion. Think about how smart food companies give you a sample of a product. You walk through a store and they have a special on a nice roast. They slice that roast up into little bitty pieces and offer you a sample. If you taste it and like it, that taste sticks with you. It makes you turn back and look at the price, take a coupon, and perhaps purchase a roast you had no intention of buying. All because you got a little taste of it and you liked it. Exposure works just like that. You'll never know what you could be missing unless you open up your world and experience people, places, talents, skills, and cultures that are different than yours.

Again, your tour guides help with exposure—especially when you are careful to select a diverse group of mentors. Your tour guides have been places and done things you may have never considered. Being exposed to them can give you a taste of something different, something that might change the course of your destination. Make friends and include in your networks people who look different than you, speak a different language than yours, live in different neighborhoods than you, attended different schools, etc. Get it?

If you don't have a valued mentor, get one, two, three, and more. How? Remember teachers, advisers, cousins, church members, and relationships developed on the train, etc. Meet people. Observe them. Keep in touch with them. Rarely do people turn down an opportunity to talk about themselves, so ask questions. Find out what path they took to get where they are. Share a cup of coffee and ask a million questions. Soak up the information and expand your network.

And tour guides, while they have lots of wisdom to impart, are not always older than we are. We can learn from the young, 12-year-old tenacious entrepreneur. Parents can learn from children—how to approach the world fearlessly and without prejudice. Ever played with a child and got a new perspective on living fearlessly? Power-packed messages can come in tiny packages.

I love the story of Naomi and Ruth because it illustrates the beauty of intergenerational sharing—and learning from folks in the oddest places. You can read the entire story in the book named after one of the heroines—Ruth. But I'll break it down quickly for you here. Ruth was Naomi's daughter-in-law. Ruth had married Naomi's son when Naomi and her family had fled a famine in Bethlehem and moved to Moab. But while in the foreign country, Naomi's husband and later her two sons died. Naomi felt broken and alone and desired to return to her home land of Bethlehem. Ruth decided to go back with her mother-in-law—even though her mother-in-law told her to stay in her hometown. But Ruth insisted. You see, young Ruth had lots to impart to Naomi. She walked by her side during a dark period of her life. She accompanied her on a long journey back to her homeland. And, when the women arrived in Bethlehem, Ruth decided to go out and work to care for the two women. Ruth was a blessing to the older Naomi. And in turn, Naomi shared some wisdom with the younger Ruth. Naomi got Ruth another husband—yep, she showed her how to capture the attention of Boaz, also called a kinsmen-redeemer, or a savior and helper. When Boaz and Ruth married, they had a son, and Naomi helped take care of him. So, while she lost two sons, she said she gained lots of sons through the birth of Boaz and Ruth's child. She received another family through her younger daughter-in-law. Ruth received a man, a baby, and a place in the history of the lineage of Christ. Not a bad deal. Both women helped each other.

How can you help an older person? A younger person? On this journey, look for those who can impart knowledge to you, but also remember to share with them and others. Your gifts and experiences have given you a unique perspective—one no one else can have because they are not you. Share, network, grow, accompany on this journey of life.

Wisdom for the Journey

Help is cyclical—look for someone to mentor you and someone to mentor.

So let's agree to use all our energy in getting along with each other. Help others with encouraging words...

Romans 14:19, MSG

For I am longing to see you so that I may share with you some spiritual gift to strengthen you— or rather, that we may be mutually encouraged by each other's faith, both yours and mine.

Romans 1:11-12, NRSV

6

Travel Mates:
The Instinct to Make,
Keep and Change Friends

RIGHT ALONG WITH TOUR GUIDES, YOU HAVE YOUR travel mates—those who you've chosen to share this journey with. They are probably closer to you than your tour guides and you may talk to your travel mates more frequently. They know you better, have seen you through the ups and downs of life, and are the people you want to invite to your party. These travel mates are called friends in the journey of life. There's no doubt, friends can be so important on this adventure of life.

Let's look at the type of friends you have around you and how they can help you face your unlimited future. Your inner circle is comprised of the friends who know you the best—intimately (and that's not sexual). These are the people who've seen you without makeup, they've probably seen you have a real cry, the ugly cry. They know more about you than others—and that's why these folks need to be chosen carefully. Only people you can truly trust with your life should be allowed to enter into your inner sanctuary of life; you need to know your true blue friends have your back, will support you even during the roughest of times, and want to be with you for you—not for any other reason. Those types of friendships take some time to cultivate and some trials to overcome together. Keep this circle close to you and value them. Invest time in those who are the closest to you; care about them, support them, protect these friendships with your life and your heart.

You probably have more casual friends than inner circle friends. Casual friends are those friends with whom you probably share a common interest, a common goal, some classes together, etc. Know what you can share and what you can't with these friends. Treat them with great respect and enjoy each other's company as much as possible. But make sure they are going somewhere you want to go. I always say I want friends who can take me somewhere. I like to learn from my friends. I like to grow from my interactions with my friends. I want friends who will educate me and uplift me and inspire me.

The parable in the Bible of the paralytic man whose friends brought him to Jesus in Mark 2 shows the type of friends I want around me (Mark 2:1-5). The man couldn't walk, and his friends evidently had heard about the healing power of Jesus. They knew that if they could get their friend to Jesus, he could be healed. But, when they got to the house where Jesus was staying, it was already filled with many people. There was no room—even outside of the house—for the friends to get to Jesus and find help for the paralytic man. But these friends didn't stop. They had enough compassion for their friend and faith in Jesus to come up with another solution—they thought outside of the box and got radical. Their friends' healing meant that much to them. Instead of saying: "sorry, we couldn't get you to Jesus; the crowd was too big," these four friends tore the roof of off the house—literally—and brought their paralyzed friend to Jesus through the top of the house. They wanted their friend healed so badly that they did the unconventional, they took a risk and they made sure their friend got the help he needed.

And that's exactly what we all need—friends who will not accept no for an answer. When they encounter a road-block, they figure out a way to get help for their friend in need. Do you have friends who would tear the roof off of a house to make sure you got the help you needed? Are you willing to be that kind of a friend to the one who is in need? I know I want friends who can walk and carry a heavy load when I need them to. They will intervene for me when they know I need help. They will break protocol and do what needs to be done to get me that help.

Yes, there's something valuable about birds of a feather flocking together. I want instinct minded friends who can see what I need and do what needs to be done to get me that help. I want friends who are walking and moving and pressing toward goals. I want friends who've decided to follow their instincts and live their dreams. I need to ride with folks making the most of this journey of life. I want to ride with folks looking to grasp their unlimited future with both hands.

Check your vehicle. Who's riding with you?

If you need to upgrade and get some different friends, follow your instinct—you know who is good for you and who is not. Have the courage to release friends who are not in your best interest. In the long run, you will help yourself and just may help them see differently. You want friends who will encourage you, not discourage you. You want friends who will cheer you on when others will call you a mere dreamer. You want friends who will push you toward your goal, not hold you back. Know that some friends are in our lives for a season, a reason or a lifetime. And sometimes you have to look at the calendar and determine what season it is for what friendships. Consider where you are headed and who is best to take the journey with.

Some of the buddies from the block can't go with you into your future; they don't have the vision. Some of your college mates may not be the ones you invest lots of time in; they may not know how to lift heavy loads. They were/ are friends for a season in time and that's okay. Learn to dust your feet and move on—even when it hurts, you'll be better off in the long run. There's no need to burn bridges, curse someone out, or go off; you can be grateful for what you had and experienced together, but know that for the next leg of the journey, you will need more focused, more supportive, more visionary travel mates. Check the tickets of your friends and make sure they are traveling in your direction.

Not every break up will need a conversation. No one wants to hear: "I'm going further down the road so you'll have to get off this bus at the next stop." If you stop calling so much, hanging out so much, talking the same talk, your friends will get the message. They will realize you're not as close as you once were. They will not see you in the same places, doing the same things and eventually that connection will diminish if you're strong enough to keep going. Nastiness is not needed. You never know when they will reach your destination and could become a friend again. Don't hinder a future opportunity with a present argument or dissing.

When you look at the reason some friends are in your life, it could be for a particular season of time or a lifetime. Your lifetime friends are the ride and die, stick-with-me, support me to the end friends. Know the difference between seasonal friends and lifetime friends. Both are valuable and can travel with you—some just need to get off the bus when the season is up. Ending a season doesn't end the memories and deposits made in each other's lives.

You may also find that it is time to make new friends and welcome them as travel mates on your journey. You can make friends wherever you may be—usually around a common interest or connection. Continue to look for values you cherish in your friends. You don't need a twin or a duplicate of you, but you do want your closest pals to have similar values as you. They should be able to lift you up, support you, and even challenge you. And they too should be able to add value to your life. Friends give and take from each other; a one-sided (or lop-sided) relationship is not really a friendship.

Your friends are reflections of you and can enhance who you are. Iron sharpens iron and you can learn from and teach each other. Get some sharp people on board with you; they have much to show you. When you have friends who have differences (not necessarily different values, but perhaps different backgrounds, cultures, interests, etc.)—you see those differences as strengths, not weaknesses or contradictions. These friends help you see things through different lenses—and nothing is wrong with that.

It's okay to have friendly associates—co-workers, church members, others who you may have one common interest with and an "association" with, but don't confuse associate with friend. An associate is someone who works beside you; a friend is someone who walks with you. One you want to roll up your sleeve and get a task done with (and that's great); the other you may want to work with, but you also want to walk with—journey with, share ups and downs with; live this journey with. One you can do without once the task is over, the other you don't want to let go because they are a true travel mate.

Wisdom for the Journey
   Friends are the family we choose so choose wisely.

But a true friend sticks by you like family.

Proverbs 18:24, MSG

It's better to have a partner than go it alone. Share the work, share the wealth.
And if one falls down, the other helps, But if there's no one to help, tough!...
By yourself you're unprotected. With a friend you can face the worst.
Can you round up a third? A three-stranded rope isn't easily snapped.

Ecclesiastes 4:9-10, 12, MSG

7

The Home Front:
The Instinct to Set Up
Your Home for Success

WHEN LOOKING FORWARD AND PLANNING for success, many of us remember to check our resumes and networks, send follow-up emails and book the right appointments, but what about our home front? How do the places we live and reside in prepare us for success or failure? How do the people we choose to live with and share common space help or hinder our journey toward fulfilling our purpose and living fulfilled and successful lives?

It might just surprise you how your home life and the choices you make about the place you lay your hat can impact your strategy for success. It is just as important to follow your instinct when deciding about your domicile. Home can be the place you spend the most time in, the place where you lay down and get rest to face the jungle. Home is an important place. Let's look inside our homes and do a little assessment (and maybe cleaning) as we propel into this next stop on this journey of life.

Where do you live? Is it helpful or hurtful for your best thinking to take place. Is your home—whether it is in your parents' basement, your grandma's side room, a nice place alone or with one or more roommates—a place where you feel safe and at peace?

If it is not, it's time you make plans to move. You may not be able to pack up today, but it's important to set some plans in motion and look for a new spot or make your current space more productive and in line with what you need and want.

Your location is critical; do you live close enough to work? If not, do you have adequate and reliable transportation to get there on time? Are there grocery stores nearby that sell the type of food you need to fuel your body? Are there restaurants you like with prices you can afford? (more on what you can afford in chapter 10) What about the people in the community? Are they like-minded? Do they care about their community? Is trash strewn in your path as you walk out the door? All of these concerns can impact your outlook and mood. And when you're trying to follow your destiny, stay tuned into your instinct, and live purposefully, distractions need to be minimized as much as possible. Your environment—especially your home environment—should support your dream and give you energy to keep going on this journey. So if your outward space is less than desirable, use it as an impetus to push you to find a place that can energize you and push you on this journey.

And while helpful external forces can set the stage for your attaining your goals, the people you live with—and the energy they expend—often have more to do with your home front and how it can push you forward. A stressful roommate situation can prove challenging at best; when things are not right at home, you are not right in the office, in your creative space, in other areas of your life. You don't think as well as you could and you may be even more tempted to make decisions based on emotions not even related to the decisions at hand—that's not your best thinking and that doesn't lead to success.

When looking for a roommate, consider everything—as much as you can. When you refuse to consider all things, it is like refusing to consider anything. Does your roommate pay bills on time? Will you pay your rent together or separately? Whose name is on the lease? How will you be penalized if your roommate doesn't pay or moves out before the lease is completed?

How does your potential roommate treat property? Is his furniture damaged? What about her cleaning habits? Are they compatible with yours? Cooking, eating? Talk about everything you can think of—before you agree to move in.

Good friends don't always make good roommates, just

like great dates don't always make great mates. Choosing the roommate can foreshadow how you will chose your mate if you are single. And sharing space with a roommate can prepare you for the compromising mindset you will need to live with your wife or husband in the future. When you are used to living alone and having everything just like you want it, it can be quite daunting to have the love of your life come in with his own set of rules and ways of doing things (we'll get to love in chapter 9). So having a roommate when you are single can help you learn to compromise. It can help you realize that everyone has different sets of rules and rhythms to live by—so you learn to adjust and adapt and consider another person in your home.

And there's lots more to consider when finding your roommate. Is your roomie an early bird? Late night owl? How do you respect each other's space as well as enjoy common space and time together? What about the volume of music, television, or video games? Banging rap or calming classical music or silence? It all has to be figured out and respected—because each person deserves to have her space respected and her needs addressed. You may not get it just like you like it all the time, but you should have a home with conditions that you've agreed to and space you enjoy living in. It's the place you should relish coming back to at the end of each day. It's the place you can be yourself—even more than any other place. Your home is where you walk around without makeup, with garlic breath and uncombed hair—in old but comfortable pajamas. It's where you can be you. Are you comfortable with your roommate knowing you at that level? You should be.

Another vitally important consideration is can you trust your roommate's decisions? Smoking and drinking and drugs—what are his feelings on using these? Think about it: do you want your record and name violated because of the decisions someone else made? What if your roommate is a drug user or opens your home to her friends who use drugs? Not only are drug users untrustworthy for a boatload of reasons, but if something goes down and the cops raid your place—you are in trouble. No matter how clean you are if you are in a place with drugs, if your name is on the lease, if you are associated with the offenders, you could be liable. Do you really want to be punished just because you were in the same room or house? Do you want to be forced to halt your journey or take a detour because of the people you chose to room with? One run-in with the law can lead to a lifetime of trouble—not that it can't be overcome, but why go through that if you don't have to?

For a Biblical example on how badly "rooming" with the wrong person can go, check out the account of Amnon and his close friend Jonadab (let's call him Jon for short). Their story is in 2 Samuel 13. Amnon and Jon were apparently cousins and close enough to share secrets and to notice when one was upset. They knew when something was amiss and cared enough to try and fix the issue. Now, we all need a few friends like this—those who are up close and in our personal space. But watch out when that friend is not the wisest or not full of integrity or just wants you to "get over it and get better." That type of friend might prescribe some quick and easy fix without giving thought to future implications. Instinct isn't about quick gains and meeting current urges—it considers the long haul, the consequences.

But back to Amnon and his close buddy Jon. Amnon "loved" his half-sister Tamar, who was also David's child—by another woman. Amnon was so messed up by what he thought he wanted, he looked sick. He got all frustrated and bothered. Well, Jon asked Amnon what was wrong and Amnon explained that he "loved" Tamar. Jon had an easy fix; he had a way to get Amnon back to being his buddy who wasn't all hot and bothered. He suggested Jon fix the problem—not by asking his father for Tamar's hand so he could make her his bride. Jon suggested that Amnon come up with a way to be left alone with Tamar so he could fix his problem. Jon's plan worked—Amnon asked his father to have Tamar come to his room and make him food. When they were alone, Amnon grabbed

Tamar and raped her. He got what he wanted—thanks to the advice of Jon. Now, even if you are not familiar with this story, I don't have to tell you that it doesn't end well for anyone involved. After Amnon takes his sister by force, he decides he doesn't love her, but hates her. He has disgraced Tamar because he was obsessed with her beauty to the point of sickness—and listened to someone who gave him a quick fix for the cure. Tamar became a refugee; her brother Absalom was so upset, he eventually killed Amnon for what he did to Tamar and Absalom even tried to wrestle the kingdom from David. Amnon's decision—planted by his buddy Jon—led to one awful consequence after another. What would have happened if Amnon had friends with integrity? What advice would he have been given? How could this story have had a different ending and how many of its players would have been able to use their gifts and talents for good rather than evil?

Amnon and Jon remind us that those who are in our inner circle—including those we choose to live with—are critical to helping us live instinctively. You may be strong and you may have your head on straight, but don't sleep on the power of other influences, especially those with less integrity than you. The way they see it, you should go for what you want—by any means necessary. And we all know that they won't be around when the consequences (or anything else) hits the fan. Just a little bit of gas can set the house on fire and your life ablaze.

Choose wisely. Choose like-minded people, or better yet, people you can learn from and grow with.

Now many of you who are starting out on this journey as adults need to live with parents or grandparents—it's the sign of the times. Salaries are lower and the cost of housing is on the increase. Set the ground rules with them too. Now that you are an adult, you and your parents should have different expectations than you had when you were a child.

A sign of maturity and responsible adulthood is taking care of your own—in whatever way that might mean. If your mama still does your laundry, will you expect her to do it when you are married or move out? Do you pay her for doing a chore you should take care of?

Remember that each task comes at a cost.

Do you live with an elderly person—or another—who needs help? What is expected? When? How can you pay with your help—also known as sweat equity. Sometimes the best pay can be through tasks we help with; find out what is needed and be of assistance.

Needing to live with your folks is nothing to be ashamed of—unless you're taking advantage of them. This can be the perfect set up to help you save money to secure your own place or the things you need to secure your place.

But have a plan. Have a timeline and try to stick to it. Instinct knows when it is time to go and doesn't over-stay her welcome. And surely your dreams are beyond the walls of your mama's house.

Wisdom for the Journey

Stay calm; mind your own business; do your own job. You've heard all this from us before, but a reminder never hurts. We want you living in a way that will command the respect of outsiders, not lying around sponging off your friends.

1 Thessalonians 4:11-12, MSG

8

Farewell:

The Instinct to Move from Dependent to Independent Status

HAVE YOU EVER JUST SAT BACK AND THOUGHT about the cycle of life? Whether looking at the animal kingdom or the human species, God's plans are just mind-blowing and very orderly. The butterfly doesn't start off her journey as colorful and gorgeous—a sight to behold. She begins as an egg and lives for a time as a creepy, little, green caterpillar, complete with as many as 16 legs. The caterpillar crawls and grows and finds food to eat. Perhaps unknowingly, she is getting ready for something grand and large and celebrated, but she must go through each stage, one step at a time. After she eats all she can as a caterpillar, it is then time for the transition phase where she forms a hard shell to hide away in and develop the essential parts to become a butterfly. From the pupa stage emerges the creature we admire—the beautiful butterfly, who commands must of us to stand in awe and at attention when we are lucky enough to catch a glance of one fluttering around.

Likewise, our life cycle has phases—each vitally important to helping us blossom and grow into all we were created to be. As an embryo, each of us is fed for nine months and kept comfortable and secure inside of our mother's womb. At the right time, the baby comes out and does nothing more than eat, sleep, poop and stare off into space wondering why so many of us are making googly eyes at him. In time, teeth develop and the babe can eat a little food. Eventually, he learns to crawl and walk and talk and throw a ball. Each stage has new adventures, new tasks, and new sets of rules the child learns to adapt to.

And so does life.

As a graduate, you've successfully navigated through some stages of life. You've completed some requirements and have been deemed ready for another stage. As an adult, you can say goodbye to some of the things you did as a child (or as a younger adult). You put on different clothes and walk a different way in this stage. And one of the most challenging things you have to figure out how to do is to help those who've raised you know that you are in another stage. Sometimes you have to help parents and grandparents and older brothers and sisters know how to cut the apron strings; how to say *hasta la vista, baby* to the old you and hello to the older, more mature person you've become.

It would be detrimental if a toddler kept sucking on a bottle after he has several teeth. She might like milk and her mother might like giving it to her, but truthfully, to continue to grow and thrive, a child needs more than milk. Her teeth need to be sharpened, which comes from chewing on something harder than apple sauce. Your decision-making abilities need to be sharpened too, and if mama's still making every decision for you, you're not going to develop and be able to live as an independent adult. Likewise, if you're allowing someone else to make all of your decisions, you are stunting your growth and jeopardizing your independent status.

The jungle of life can be scary, but you have been pre-pared through each stage of life. Now is the time to put that preparation into practice and fly. You won't know that you can until you do it. You have your instincts, your intellect, and your God; take the leap to fully live this life as you were designed to. The adult stage of life can be the best part of your life; it's where you get to make the de-cisions and live with the consequences—isn't this what every child waits for? This stage of life can be filled with many blessings and lessons.

What's your plan for the adult stage of life? How are you growing closer to the independent role? Do you still rely on others to make your decisions? How can you let go? How can you have confidence in your training and take a leap of faith to stand on your own two feet. You can do it. Your instincts can guide you.

Set some boundaries with those well-meaning people who may still treat you like you are a child. Let them know you have plans and will be taking steps to get to them. You appreciate all they've done for you in the past and all they have deposited into your life. Now, it's time to live off of those lessons and to learn some new ones— on your own. (Remember this comes at a cost—and some of it is financial. A grown person who makes his own decisions doesn't rely financially on another person; if you're still depending on pops to pay your car note, you may need to understand that payment comes at a cost. He can tell you how to drive, where to drive, and how to take care of the car. His money comes at a cost. You have to do some cutting of the strings, too.) When you are ready to pay your own way through life, you can expect others to treat you as an adult and can decide if you'll still be around them if they refuse to accept (and respect) your independence.

The people who raised you are also going through another stage in life—relinquishing a dependent. Many folks feel a certain amount of value in being a caretaker. They like having someone depend on them and feel valued when they have dependents. Recognize this for what it is and set boundaries about what you will and will not allow. Advice can be welcomed, but not forced. A listening ear can be comforting, but shouldn't be nosy and meddlesome. And let's face it. You're not going to do everything just like someone else did or expects you to. You are unique. You were created to be you and live the life laid before you, not someone else. You are unique and distinct and need to stand on that and find your path. Even when you fall, you are still responsible for getting up—with God's help—dusting yourself off and moving forward. Some of the best lessons are learned when you fall down (more on that in Chapter 11). But if you're still using training wheels on a bike, you're less likely to fall— and less likely to ever want to take those wheels off and learn to ride on your own. Training wheels are meant to teach you how to ride the bike without them—they were not meant to be a permanent part of your bike-riding experience. Use your own wings and fly in your own world.

Take a look at the portrait of the woman described in Proverbs 31 (verses 10-31). Whether you are a man or a woman, these verses can give you some insight on how a fully grown person lives. She's flying in full adulthood mode and can show us all some things about being grown. She is industrious—she makes things happen. She's not sitting around waiting for money to drop out of the sky. Neither is she relying on her husband to take care of everything, as if he is her daddy (or sugar daddy). In fact, the Scripture says she is a help to her husband and he can trust her. She enhances his life—and all of those who come in contact with her. She gets up early and stays up late to take care of what she has to get done. She's not making excuses or taking short cuts. She steps up to her responsibilities and handles them. She's wise—she considers what she needs before she makes purchases. She's an investor—she makes profits. And while she uses her talents to help her family and to increase, she doesn't forget about those in need. She's some woman. She's a grown woman and she acts like it.

Many have debated if we should try to live up to this amazing Proverbs 31 woman. I definitely think we should use her as a model for living as adults—whether we can be superwoman or superman like she seems to be or not. Read about her to gain more insight on living independently and grown up.

The truly independent person also understands the concept of interdependence. This means that yes, I am responsible and strong and taking care of my business, but I also recognize that I need others and others need me. I am reliable and responsible enough to lend a helping hand—and I am wise and humble enough to ask for help when I need it. A person who can't ask for help—or take help when it is given—will find himself in a tough and lonely spot. We are not islands. We were meant to live in community and interdependently. Take care of your business—but keep an eye on your brother too. You are your brother and sister's keeper. And don't feel you can go throughout this life without being the one needing a little help sometimes. What a relief it can be to have a much needed helping hand by your side.

A true adult knows that she is not in this world alone nor designed and created to be alone (Genesis 2:18-20). Asserting your independence is a critical step and important phase of life, but learning that you are interdependent takes even more maturity. No, you can't do it alone. You may want to sometimes, you may feel like you are sometimes, but in the end, you need your neighbor, you need some friends, you need God's help to make it through. So in this do-it-your-self world of strong, independent people, remember to depend on others and be dependable for others who need a hand. You will be much stronger as you lean on God's unchanging hand—and a friend's helping hand.

Wisdom for the Journey

When I was a child, I spoke like a child, I thought like a child, I reasoned like a child; when I became an adult, I put an end to childish ways.

1 Corinthians 13:11, NRSV

The Holy Spirit produces this kind of fruit in our lives: love, joy, peace, patience, kindness, goodness, faithfulness, gentleness, and self-control. There is no law against these things!

Galatians 5:22-24, NLT

9

The Hunt for Love:
The Instinct to Find
Lifelong Love

WELL, SINCE WE'VE ESTABLISHED THAT THIS LIFE is not meant to be lived alone—what about your mate? Yes, marriage is one way you can live with someone and partner with them on this journey of life. While that significant other doesn't replace God or your friends or other families, having a true life partner can be a sweet way to enjoy this journey of life.

But there are important steps an instinct follower takes when pursuing love.

First, it's important to be honest with yourself and ask: are you ready for life-long love? Are you ready to settle down and set up a home with your husband or wife? Do you have the skills it will take to run a household and care for another, perhaps even children? The easy answer is: yes, but what does it really mean to be ready for love?

I'm not asking if you are ready for lust? I'm not asking you if you're ready to be coupled with a beautiful person and enjoy great dinners and trips together. No, love runs deeper than that—at least it should if you don't want to end up in divorce court.

So start with yourself; ask if you're ready for love, not lust. Love in marriage, as established in Ephesians 5, is really a reflection of God's love for us. And we know God gave Jesus for us so that's some pretty sacrificial love. Are you willing and ready to be self-sacrificing? Can you joyfully put another's needs and wants and desires ahead of yours? It's not as bad as it sounds, but it is as serious as it sounds. You see, when you put your mates needs in front of yours and she puts your needs in front of hers, you have a win-win situation. You have two people loving each other unconditionally, supporting each other—even when it is hard. That is a beautiful thing, but it's not necessarily easy or natural. It takes mature, committed people following God's leading to do it and to do it well—then you wake up the next morning and do it all over again. Talk about a journey.

One of the reasons marriages fail is because people are not honest about who they are when they are dating. If you are looking for true love, look for the real person, not the representative who shows up on the date. Look beyond the makeup and clothes to the heart and the motives and the person inside. You want to wake up each morning next to a real person, a person you love and like and respect. In the end, that's what we all want: to be loved for who we are. And that's some serious love.

So, it is perfectly okay to say you're not ready for that

type of commitment. Maybe you already know you're too focused on starting your own business or you want certain things before you devote time and energy to a mate. Perhaps you have some deep-seated issues that need to be dealt with before you can give out or even receive true love—do you know how to forgive? Have you forgiven others in your past? Can you communicate your needs and wants well? What lessons have you learned from your parents' relationships—whether good or bad? Have you come to terms with what you would like to emulate and what you would like to do differently than they did? All of these areas can be worked on and strengthened while you get ready for your lifelong mate. And if you know you're not ready or have some major issues to work on first, be honest with the folks you encounter. Don't lead them to believe they could be the next Mr. or Mrs. for you. Say you're not even in the game right now. Dating for dating sake should be done amongst like-minded people. And dating for mating should be done between like-minded, equally yoked folk (2 Corinthians 6:14)

And on that note, if you are looking to marry Mr. Right, stop dating Mr. Wrong. If you're looking to get married and enjoy this ride with a life-long partner, stop dating women who just look like they will be good for you as long as the money is around. As sure as life is here, times will change. What you have today will not always be here—and that can be good and bad. Lifelong partners are in it for life, for the long haul. They are not in it as long as you can take them on trips or to nice restaurants. They want to be with you the person, not you the title or you the look or you the money. Do you know how to weed out people who are looking for the right-now man or the good-time girl? Can you spot out potential lifetime mates—people who are genuinely interested in getting to know you and walking with you and loving you like Christ loves the church? It makes me excited just thinking about those types of people—that's what you want for a lifelong mate. You want someone you see yourself growing old with, holding your hand when things get rough, enjoying conversations and supporting each other to be the best you can be.

Make your lifelong mate your friend, the one you want to run to and tell how your day was; the one you want to cry in his arms; the one you want to stay up late helping figure out a problem. That doesn't always come in a neat outside package labeled: lifelong mate. It comes from listening to the person's heart; studying the person's lifestyle, friends and family. Hearing his goals and watching how he pursues them can give you insight into who he is. Observing how she lets her light shine in the dark now can show you how she will let it shine in the future with you.

When you are on the hunt for love, you've got lots to be looking out for—and most of it isn't in words. It is in actions and interactions with co-workers, friends, even enemies. Keep both eyes open when hunting. You're going to need to see what you're signing up for and who you are signing up with. Lifelong love is a beautiful thing that is developed and nurtured and watered to grow into a beautiful flower.

Lifelong love takes a commitment to make it work. It reminds me of when older people used to make new dishes out of whatever ingredients they had in the pantry. If they went to make cornbread and they didn't have flour, they made hot water corn bread, which doesn't need flour. If they only had leftovers, they made gumbo. Some great delicacies came from making it work—and likewise, some powerful, life-sustaining love can come from people who want to make it work and will do what they need to do to make it work. Are you ready?

Read Ephesians 5:21-33 for God's expectations of husbands and wives. It begins with reminding each person to be respectful of each other. And it reminds couples to be supportive and loving, not abusive or overpowering. Husbands and wives are on this journey together. They are riding together in the same direction on this journey. When they adopt the love of Christ into their marriage and pick up some make-it-work commitment, they can enjoy a beautiful trip together.

If you are on the hunt for love, look for someone you can work together with to enjoy this journey. Invest your energy in people who are good traveling mates for this journey. Invest in people who can get you to your destiny, not distract you from it. The dating game can get tricky; keep your eyes on the prize and your goals.

True love lets you be you. And that's what you need to look for when choosing a mate. Do you know who the person is? Do you know who is under the makeup and Gucci suit? Do you know what's in his heart? What drives him? What is she like when she is upset? What is her moral center like? How's his integrity? Some questions to answer before you say "I Do."

Wisdom for the Journey

No one abuses his own body, does he? No, he feeds and pampers it. That's how Christ treats us, the church, since we are part of his body. And this is why a man leaves father and mother and cherishes his wife. No longer two, they become "one flesh." This is a huge mystery, and I don't pretend to understand it all. What is clearest to me is the way Christ treats the church. And this provides a good picture of how each husband is to treat his wife, loving himself in loving her, and how each wife is to honor her husband.

Ephesians 5:29-33, MSG

Love never gives up.
Love cares more for others than for self.
Love doesn't want what it doesn't have.
Love doesn't strut,
Doesn't have a swelled head,
Doesn't force itself on others,
Isn't always "me first,"
Doesn't fly off the handle,
Doesn't keep score of the sins of others,
Doesn't revel when others grovel,
Takes pleasure in the flowering of truth,

INSTINCT FOR GRADUATES

Puts up with anything,
Trusts God always,
Always looks for the best,
Never looks back,
But keeps going to the end.

1 Corinthians 13: 4-7, MSG

10

Travel Fund:
The Instinct to Spend,
Save, and Increase

A S YOU TRAVEL ALONG THE ROAD OF LIFE, THERE'S something you need for sure—a travel fund. Money is our currency and knowing how to make money, save money, invest money and spend money wisely is an important tool on the ride of your life. If you expect to face your unlimited future, you will need to know how to handle the dollars. This is not about getting filthy rich or wealthy for wealth sake, this is more about being a good steward of what God has put into your possession. It's about being grateful for your gifts and talents and the ability to make money—so when you are grateful, you say thank you and act like you mean it. Handling your money instinctively is yet another way of thanking God for the gifts placed inside of you.

So let's get down to some money management basics to help you live a fruitful future.

A big word that is often neglected today is budget. Yes, everyone benefits from living on a budget—from Warren Buffet on down to the full-time student. When you know how much you have to spend for a certain amount of time—and do it—you are successfully living on a budget. And this type of discipline flows into other areas of your life. When you can resist overspending, you can resist doing a lot of other unhealthy and negative things—like overeating, overindulging, over anything. A balanced budget often equals a balanced life—a person positioned to benefit from instinctive living.

So how do you get there? I know not everyone is born with the innate sense to live within their means. Our culture has turned material goods into a mini god. We want flashy cars, great clothes, the latest technology—and we want these trinkets now. But wise instinct followers understand that they can't get everything they want right now. They know the difference between what they need and what they want. They use their money and budget to pay for their needs—and they develop a savings plan to get some of their wants. If there's an item you really, really want, waiting for it won't hurt you. In fact, it could help you decide if you really want it. Waiting could also give you the impetus and time to research the cost and figure out a way to buy your desired item for less than expected.

Look at your current budget. How much money do you bring home each week, two-weeks, or monthly after taxes? That is the money you have to live on, not the dollar amount they quote you when you are hired. When you make $25,000 a year or $10 an hour, you don't get to take home that amount. After you pay the IRS, social security and other deductions, you end up taking home less. So know what your real take-home amount is before you start to budget. Then know your steady expenses; the things that won't change from month-to-month. These are also considered needs so you *need* to pay them on time. (rent, utilities, loans, etc.) I am a firm believer in giving God a percentage of our income—it's the least we can do to say thank you. So, set aside the amount you will give to God (10 percent is a tithe). Many people take that amount right off the top of their pay so they won't be tempted to spend it when they get down to the small change. Learning to tithe now when you may not make six figures is a good idea. Then when you have more money, 10 percent of your income won't feel like a burden. You'll be used to giving it. Remember, God doesn't need our money so you're not doing God a favor when you set aside a tithe. Tithing is more about how we feel about God rather than if God needs our money. If I feel I can trust God, if I feel thankful for what God has done for me and in me, I want to give and give freely. It's about your attitude.

I like to think about the ten lepers when I think about my attitude toward God. This story is in Luke 17:11-19. Ten men had the contagious and unclean disease called leprosy. Their skin was probably covered with sores and they could have experienced muscle pain. In Biblical times, lepers were not allowed to mingle with people; they were isolated. But when these ten lepers heard that Jesus was in town, they asked him to have mercy on them and to heal them. Jesus did. He told them they were healed and they should go show themselves to the priest, who would investigate and declare them safe to enter society again. When the 10 lepers left Jesus to go to the priest, their skin began to change, demonstrating that they were healed. Nine of the lepers kept walking and headed to the priest to be declared clean. But one man, when he realized just what had occurred, he turned around and told Jesus thank you. We don't know why the other 9 kept on their journey; perhaps they just wanted to be declared clean so they could go on with their lives. Isolation had to be terrible for them. But, the one man was so thankful for what happened that he stopped to acknowledge the healer and the way-maker, Jesus. He knew it was not possible for his leprosy to be healed without Jesus' help. He wanted to say thank you. To me, that's what we do when we obediently give of our income to help God's church and God's people; it shows we are thankful and grateful. Adding a tithe to your budget can help you say thank you, too.

Often when you look at your budget on paper (or on a screen), you may realize that you don't have enough money in your month; in other words, you don't have enough money coming in this month to cover all 28, 30 or 31 days. Bills add up and can be more than the amount of money you're bringing home. When that is the case, it's not a time to ignore your budget or bury your head in the sand or take out the credit cards. It's time to make adjustments. What can you do to lower the amount of bills you have? Are there some things that are not necessary that you can cut back on—even if for just a while? (Cable, internet, other services may seem like necessities if you've had them all of your life, but there are ways around them. And again, you're not saying you will never have these luxuries, you're just forgoing some of them to get your budget back in order. When your circumstances change, you can add them back).

Another way to help balance that budget is to get more revenue. Climbing the ladder at work and getting a raise may take longer than you want, but you could look at additional jobs (seasonal work can add some cash to your bottom line). Or perhaps you have a service you can offer to make additional money—do you bake a mean cake everyone is always requesting? Do you sew, make alterations, create, write, edit, know how to take care of kids or elders or people with special needs? Tap into your instincts and get creative. You've got a gift. You can make some money.

Another reason to have your expenses tally up to less than your income is so that you can save money. When thinking of saving, think about setting up an emergency fund—when something happens, you can go into this account and withdraw money for the accident or incident. It keeps your budget in check because you don't have to use your monthly money for an unexpected expense. Living like this can be much less stressful than robbing Peter to pay Paul. The catch up game takes energy that you could use being creative and utilizing your gifts. Get free so you can live freely.

In addition to an emergency fund, set up a retirement savings account. Take advantage of what they call free money in your company's 401K. Starting at a young age, putting away a mere 3-5 percent of your income (or more if you can) can make a world of a difference when you reach retirement age. It's a great tax benefit too—often times you won't notice a big difference in your take home pay if you contribute to the 401K (because it is pre-tax dollars it "feels" like less on your net income). Knowing the tax laws can be a bonus when finding ways to save money. Getting started early gives your money time to grow.

I mentioned credit earlier, but I'm convinced people don't know the true value of good credit until they go to make a big purchase and can't. Have you ever been turned down for a car loan? Or been required to have a co-signer? Or given an obscenely high interest rate just so you could purchase a $20,000 car? It makes you want to weep, especially when you know there's a different way. Your credit score determines so much. Banks and other companies have access to it. They basically rate your ability to pay back a loan based on your score. And there are some times you will need loans. Some purchases, like homes, come with loans. And the difference in your credit score can literally mean the difference in hundreds of dollars each month. Do you really want the fact that you didn't pay a bill—or didn't pay it on time—to stop you from living in the home or the neighborhood you desire to live in? Or to stop you from getting the job or a promotion? Or to keep you from getting your business loan to put your vision into action?

Learn early to take care of your credit. Pay your bills early and at the very least on time. Check your credit report and dispute any discrepancies. And follow through. If you owe someone and can't pay them right now—for whatever reason—pick up the phone and talk to them. It's always easier for a company to set up a payment plan for you than to make your account go into collections and have to track you down later for money. If all you can pay is $25 a month, pay that and pay it consistently. People and companies will work with you, but you've got to speak up.

Integrity steps in here. A person who takes care of his finances is usually a person who can be trusted. Look at the parable of talents (Matthew 25:14-30). The master gave one person ten talents, or money or gifts; the other five, and the last person one talent. The person with ten invested and made more, and so did the one with five. But the person with just one talent, buried it and made excuses. He was later punished while the one who did the most with his was rewarded. Regardless of where you start in life—regardless of how much more or little money you have, you can work with it. You can invest it and make it grow. You can use your gifts to the best of your ability—and get God's help for the rest! You can increase. You were created to increase—spiritually and financially. Don't bury that one talent or feel inadequate. Use what you've got and work it. Use what you've got to get what you want—careful planning, a little self-control, and some wisdom can get you there.

And, in today's day and age, it's more than likely you'll have debt for your education (also known as student loans). With the rising cost of education, many students find taking out loans is the only way to finance their education. Student loan debt can be seen as an investment.

You borrow money to improve yourself—by way of receiving a degree or special certification. You expect to get a job that pays enough for you to pay off your loans within a set time. If you find yourself with student loans, set up a reasonable pay schedule. Most lenders will work with you to pay back less in the early stages of your career and more later (when you can expect to make more money). Paying your loan on time is critical to keeping your credit score high, which helps in other areas. If you are consistent about paying your student loans, you will pay them off. You don't add more debt to them—like you can credit cards—unless you go back to school and continue to invest in yourself. If this is the case, research your intended field of study to make sure you can find a job making enough money to pay your loans consistently. Just like with any other loan, be wise, research interest rates and know what is expected of you. It's a good idea not to have a repayment penalty (that means the institution charges you for repaying the entire loan early); you want the freedom to be able to pay off a loan if you get a lump sum of money and have already invested in yourself through savings. If your interest rate is low, you may consider putting that lump sum in an interest-bearing savings account that will give you more money than you'd save paying off the loan. It's a numbers game. Read and understand the numbers in order to play the game wisely.

How are you treating your money? Are you saying "thank you" for all you've been given?

Wisdom for the Journey

Whoever sows generously will also reap generously. Each of you should give what you have decided in your heart to give, not reluctantly or under compulsion, for God loves a cheerful giver. And God is able to bless you abundantly, so that in all things at all times, having all that you need, you will abound in every good work.

2 Corinthians 9:6-8, NIV

Give away your life; you'll find life given back, but not merely given back—given back with bonus and blessing. Giving, not getting, is the way. Generosity begets generosity.

Luke 6:38, MSG

11

*You've Got This:
The Instinct to Survive
the Dark*

I AM CONVINCED THAT ONE OF THE MAJOR ELEMENTS that separates the successful person from the average, mediocre along-for-the-ride type of person is how they handle adversity. It boils down to one simple word: perspective. An instinct driven person sees a storm, challenge or dark time as an opportunity, while the other person sees a difficult time as that—a storm, a problem, and a crisis. Let me be clear, no matter who you are, how you look, what school you graduated from, who your parents are (you get me?), you will meet up with some adversity. Life will get dark. There will definitely be some stormy nights (and days for that matter). This journey is just that—a journey— and it is filled with some ups and some downs. Our goal is to push past those dark times and not let them count us out or get us down or make us give up hope. And instinct followers see these dark times like a student sees the classroom or a scientist sees the lab. It's time to learn something new and exciting that will position us for the next blessing, the next breakthrough, the next level.

The difference is perspective. Instinct followers see challenges and hard times as opportunities. Yep, no matter how hard it gets, how rough it is, how horrific it is, they somehow find the strength and the perspective to see it as an opportunity. Sometimes it takes extra time, sometimes it takes even more prayers and interventions, but in the end, instinct followers know they will get through the dark and see the light again. They keep pushing and moving and looking for the opportunity.

Let's look deeper at the perspective of an instinct follower when life gets dreary and dark.

Again, a single word can be used to sum things up. This time it is: focus. Whatever you focus on grows. Whatever you give attention to becomes important. Imagine being at a large venue with a famous person. The moment that famous person walks up to someone and shakes her hand, that person becomes important. Why? Because the star gave that person some attention. Paparazzi want to know who they are, cameras click and take that person's picture. Because she got attention, she is important.

Problems work the same way. The more attention and focus you give your problems, the more important they become. The more dominant they become—even seeming overwhelmingly large. Now, some problems need attention—in order for you to find a solution or to take care of them. But they don't take up your total being. When someone meets you and asks your name: you don't immediately become your problem (or you shouldn't). You are still John, the instinct follower, by the way. I'm not "I need rent money." I'm not "my girlfriend broke up with me." I'm not "I just lost my job." But we all know people who are totally consumed with their challenges and dark times. They become those things instead of being themselves and focusing on their destiny. They become their problems.

But John the instinct follower is not overly consumed by the dark. Instead his tune might sound a little something like this: "Yes, I've lost a job, but a new one must be on the way. Do you have one? Do you know of one? I'm going to interview everyone I know because they just might have one." An instinct follower's perspective is not about the problem, it's about the solution. It's about the opportunity. A lost job means there is another one to gain. No money means I'm about to get creative with what God has given me and find a way to make some money.

Yes, instinct followers know how to tap into creativity. And I think we get even more creative when we need to look inward for help. Often the complexity of our lives spawns the creativity in our lives; our instincts can cut through the clutter of chaos and forge a clear path for us to follow—that is if we're listening and are courageous enough to follow.

My ancestors were challenged to make a brutally difficult situation bearable and from that came spirituals, blues, quilts, gumbo and freedom. Many enslaved persons saw opportunity in the midst of craziness and darkness and hopelessness. What if they would have stopped hoping and focused on the problem instead of solutions and methods to sustain themselves in the dark?

As children often boredom or lack of toys—especially before the technology boom—we often used our imagination. Many a company or gadget or story has been developed in the dark room of a child's imagination because he or she didn't have money to go to Disneyland or didn't have friends to play with or his parents were too busy to play with him. The average person sits back and complains; the innovator sees it as a time to create and observe and learn and imagine. Oh, to have the perspective of an innovator.

What are you facing today? How are you seeing it—as an overwhelmingly dark obstacle that cannot be overcome or as an opportunity for you to stir up some creativity mixed in with prayer and guidance to produce something new, something you never would have thought about before.

Look at what happened when the disciples encountered a storm in Mark 4:35-39. Yes, it was a real live storm. Their boat was rocking, the waves were crashing in on them and their friend and teacher Jesus was laying in the cut just sleeping in the back of the boat (he even had a nice pillow to rest his head; he wasn't scared.) How could he sleep through a storm? That's what the disciples wanted to know. They asked Jesus: "Don't you care about us?" What irony. These men were asking Jesus, God himself, if he cared? They were asking the creator of the water and the wind why he wasn't worried about the wind? Huh? Jesus stood up and simply spoke to the storm and said: "Peace. Be Still" And he turned to the disciples and asked what was wrong with them—did they not have faith?

Those of us who believe in the power of God must believe that our dark nights will end. If we believe that God truly predestined us, then that means we must be able to get to our intended end. If my intended end is to live out my purpose and function, then I must be able to do it—no matter what is in the way or who tries to block it. People or circumstances or dark nights might be able to push me to my destiny, but they cannot block me. My energy is better spent on being creative, on looking for my next step toward my destiny. I'm in a better mood if I do like Jesus and get a little rest while my storm is going on (you know being tired makes it all seem worse!). I'll do better if I focus on the opportunity rather than the issue—no matter what it is.

Learn to filter adversity through your instinct to survive. Every obstacle contains an opportunity. It may not be the doorway to success you were looking for—it may be a second story window left open just a crack! Even if what you've been given is wrapped in nothing but problems, these barriers can become breakthroughs; they are just blessings camouflaged as burdens, creek beds from which you will develop oceans, backyard trips that will eventually open your mind to safaris. Rarely do you have everything you think you need, but you still keep moving, expecting it all to work out.

The more you experience a night, the more you should realize morning is a coming. The first time a child sees dark, he should be afraid. That's what night lights are designed for—to help children who are afraid of the dark. But as that child gets older, he should know: morning is a coming. I might have to go to the bed in the dark, but soon it will be a new day and I will get up and play some more. The more tests and challenges and storms you see in your life, you should be able to take a look back and remind yourself that you made it out of the last one. You figured out a way to make it happen then. A new revenue stream came along the last time you were in need. A new idea came into existence the last time you were at the end of your rope—so why would this time be any different? Why fret? Get some rest, you are going to need it when morning shows up. Look for the opportunity and thank God for each step of this amazing journey. It's wild out there, but you've got what it takes to get through. You've got this.

Your instincts naturally create a way forward out of whatever you have at hand. Hardship can humble you, but it cannot break you unless you let it. Your instinct for survival will see you through if you're attuned to its frequency. It is so comforting to remember that we're equipped by what's within us to respond to the demands of what's around us at any given time.

Wisdom for the Journey

Weeping may last through the night, but joy comes with the morning.

Psalm 30:5, NLT

My brothers and sisters, whenever you face trials of any kind, consider it nothing but joy, because you know that the testing of your faith produces endurance; and let endurance have its full effect, so that you may be mature and complete, lacking in nothing.

James 1:2-4, NRSV

12

The Call of the Wild:
The Instinct to Serve
Freely

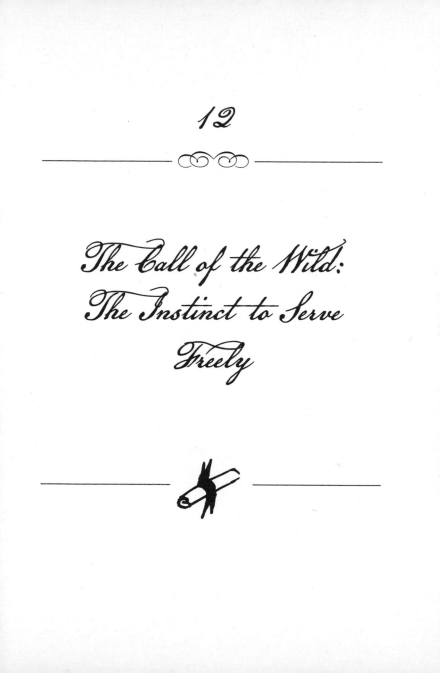

ON THIS JOURNEY TOWARD FULFILLING AND successful living, instinct chasers know that service is a direct link to their success. They understand that every good and perfect gift comes from God—including all gifts and talents and opportunities. Therefore, giving back, helping others and serving in many different capacities is instinctively a part of their lives.

I think of it this way: when you are grateful and thankful for all you have—and that means more than dollars and cars and houses—you recognize that a part of saying thank you is taking care of others. When you are grateful for this life and for the inborn drive that propels you to greatness and to your destiny, you want to take care of God's children.

Instinct followers understand their gifts—and their very being—come directly from God. They see their instincts as the personal handiwork God has placed inside of them. They recognize that while instinctive, heart-felt living pulls from the center, it does not rely solely on their own insight. It connects to God and relies on God. And when you help people based on your God-given talents, you acknowledge the One who made you—the one in whom you move and have your very being (Acts 17:28).

Giving of who you are through service to others is more about your attitude than how much you have, how talented you are and what you give. An attitude of gratitude gladly serves and shares. An attitude of gratitude recognizes that this gift is just that—a gift from above. And when you've been given something, you want to share. You want others to experience what you have experienced. And you know the value of having basic needs—and even some wants—met. How do you say thank you: you serve and you give. You may never get anything from the people you help (and nor should you expect to), but you've already received so much from God and others. Say thank you. Serve someone today.

To whom much is given, much is expected. And those who give freely of their time, talents and resources (now that's money), they often find that they receive more. The cycle of giving is powerful and sometimes unexplainable. You write a check to help someone who is struggling, you get a big break. You give of your time—although you are tired and have little energy left—to help tutor a child and somehow you get an extra boost of energy or your deadline is extended or your boss is sick the day it is due. Not totally explainable or measurable, but it has to do with the fact that giving makes you free. It frees you from thinking you've gotten everything you have on your own. It frees you from thinking you operate in a silo and are isolated. It connects you in an amazing way to God and God's people. Serving feels good—and it helps others.

Sometimes when you show up to take care of others, you end up getting the treat and the gift. Sure, the person at the food bank might get the meal or the homeless family might get the new house, but you too gain some things. You gain a new perspective—those storms you are enduring don't match up with someone who doesn't have a house—let me tell you! When you see a child who doesn't have a nutritious meal, the food you have in your cupboard—whether or not it is the finest and best or what you want—just seems better and tastes better. Your perspective broadens and you are more appreciative. And we know what happens when you appreciate what you have: you take better care of it, you become a better steward, you pay attention to the instincts—and look out, you grow, you succeed, you increase. It is a win-win.

Why do some people not serve? They think they do not have it all yet so they have nothing to give or share. They think they don't have enough time, enough money or enough talent. But serving begins with you and where you are now. Your gifts may not be in the same proportion or dimension or same degree as your neighbor, but that's fine. You're not called to compete with everyone else. You're not called to use others as the barometer for your success and your level of help to others. You're called to maximize the fullness of what God has uniquely entrusted to you. It's not a race with the rest of the world. It's your journey, your course. Are you willing to give what you have? Share what you've got. You have much to give—regardless of what it looks like. And, much is expected from those who have much. Your gift isn't just for you; it's for others. Be creative, listen to your instinct to determine when and where to use it. And don't be stingy. Give it freely. You will be surprised how things open up for you.

Look at the example of the woman in Luke 21:1-4. Jesus noticed her offering, which was really just two mites or just about two pennies. Even during the time of the story, two pennies was not considered much especially if you were to compare it to what the rich people were putting in the collection boxes. But Jesus took note of this widow. We don't know how much the others put in—their amounts are not recorded in biblical accounts. But this woman's amount was; her story is recorded for everyone to know and consider. The two pennies meant more than the mighty amounts the rich contributed. Why? Because it was all she had. When you give out of the wealth of what you have, that really doesn't take much effort. To give the needy your extra is nice, but it isn't a sacrifice (and anyone can do that). What happens when you give out of what you too think you need? You give that extra hour when you're very tired; you find a way to contribute to the cause you believe in even though your money is not flowing like you'd like it; you stop and take a break to help a kid although you feel you really need to keep doing your own work—that's giving out of your lack, or need. And that is noticed.

I'm not saying you should give your rent money to the poor or stress yourself out and always give extra hours, but I think the attitude you have when you give makes the difference. Are you more concerned about what you're losing when you give or are you more concerned about how your little bit can make a difference in someone's life—whether you see the fruits right now or not. What do you think the widow was thinking when she reached deep into her pockets and gave her two pennies? She probably wasn't thinking: "I'm going to miss my little money." She was probably thinking: "I'm so grateful just to be here; I want to show just how thankful I am by finding something, anything I have, to give." Do you have that attitude? Strive to live gratefully and serve freely.

Freeing yourself from worrying about what you have

and what you won't have if you give it away is liberating and helpful to you. Open your hands and allow what you have, what you can share, to flow out of you—and watch it multiply.

What do you have to give? What needs do you see around you? Don't think you have too little to give—it is your little that can make a difference. Focus on helping the need not on yourself. Your little bit can increase.

Connect to a cause that is dear to your heart. Have you overcome something others are still trying to overcome? How can your insight and experience help them? Are you particularly saddened by something in your community? Don't sit back, shake your head and discuss the issue with your friends—do something, anything—large or small. How can you make a difference today? Serve wildly and freely and see your world around you change. And see yourself change.

Wisdom for the Journey

Praise be to the God ... who comforts us in all our troubles, so that we can comfort those in any trouble with the comfort we ourselves receive from God.

2 Corinthians 1:3-4, NIV

13

Enjoy the Ride:
The Instinct to
Lighten Up

I KNOW THROUGHOUT THIS BOOK, WE'VE TALKED A LOT about success and achieving and reaching for your goals. You were born to live the life God has designed for you—and that's a good life, filled with purpose and fulfillment, I'm certain. And even when your road is dark and the lights seem dim on this road, you can find purpose and learn lessons as you go. But there's also something just as valuable about living instinctively—and that is balance. It's important to balance what you know through information with what you feel inside; instinct truly helps you balance information, intellect, hunches and clues to make decisions. It can also help you balance work and play. In this driven, busy, get-more and do-more world, it's important to remember to enjoy the ride, to lighten up and soak in the simple things in life. Our eyes can be so focused on the prize of success and fulfillment that work becomes our only mode. We forget to laugh, we forget to dance, we forget to enjoy the simple pleasures of life. And that, my friend, is not wise.

Check your balance. How much time do you spend working and achieving and getting closer to your goals? Is having fun a goal for you that you treat as sacredly as you do tasks on your to-do list? Don't let this life pass you by without taking the time to really smell the roses along this journey. They can be sweet and give you the energy and drive to run this race more efficiently and much more enjoyably.

A good party can give you such great memories. Have you ever woke up the next day still thinking about the food you ate last night, the conversations you had, the experience? You can't get that at a computer or a business meeting.

What about the places on your bucket list? Have you set up a plan to visit any of those places? You've achieved some success and accomplished a major goal in life, how are you rewarding yourself? If you don't have the travel funds to go abroad, consider doing something that doesn't require much money. Have you seen the water in a while? Drive to a coast or one of the big lakes in the middle of the country. Schedule a day to sit at the beach and read a book just for fun. Has your favorite author come out with a book you've been dying to read? When will you do it? When will you find the time to take a break and enjoy life. Have you heard your favorite artist perform? Save up for the ticket. Plan the experience. Many cities have outdoor concerts that are free—take in one. Try something new—a different genre of music, a new dance class, a new type of food.

Some of us will change and discover our better side when we can get away and take a break—forget about the goals and work for just a while. Balance your drive with rest and pleasure. You might discover a laugh deep in your belly you forgot about because you were achieving. You may discover a sweet part of your personality that has been buried because you've been so focused.

Taste and see that God is good (Psalm 34:8). Life is meant to be enjoyed and to be lived fully. Jesus came to give life and life more abundantly (John 10:10). This scripture doesn't just apply to living financially prosperous. It means that your soul and your spirit is filled abundantly. And I imagine that filling includes some good laughter, some great friends and some relaxation. You are not a human doing; you're a human being. So be: be happy, be carefree, be light, just sit and be and enjoy something you and only you want to do. Forget about kids, your mate, your co-workers, your goals—for a moment. What would you like to do that doesn't have anything to do with your work or mission? Doing something just for fun can make you feel more alive and give you what you need to accomplish a little more.

Companies give vacation time for a reason—and the

truly successful folk use their vacation time. They don't let their vacation days roll over into the next year or cash them in for the money. They know the value of doing little to no work for a few days in a row—or two consecutive weeks or a month—now that's living. Work toward scheduling your next vacation today. If you need to save money, put some aside. It's an investment in yourself and in your well-being.

If you don't have any extra money in this season of life, schedule a stay-cation. Visit the museums in your city—some are free, I'm sure. It's amazing how many people live in cities that people travel to from all over the world—and those locals have never discovered what the tourists are enjoying day in and day out. Get that local guide and find one place you haven't explored—or revisit a place you loved and felt alive while visiting. Search for coupons for discounts on new adventures—and try one. Get out and see your city, state, your world. You only live once.

One of the richest men to ever live was King Solomon (1 Kings 10:23). He reigned over the kingdom of Israel after his father, David. Solomon was not only rich, he was wise. He had silver, gold, clothing, weapons, spices, horses, chariots—you name it, he had the finest. But Solomon pens an interesting book in the Bible—Ecclesiastes. When you get the chance to read through Ecclesiastes, you will read Solomon's musings about life. After ruling as king of a great nation and having all of the riches and wisdom in the world, Solomon concludes that life is pretty hollow and shallow and even meaningless. After all of the working and toiling we do, what do we really have? I think Solomon was trying to encourage us to first keep God as our center and our purpose. If we run after wealth and achievement, we will find that it is not enough to sustain us or to make us happy. Solomon says: "I've concluded there is nothing better than to be happy and enjoy ourselves as long as we can. And people should eat and drink and enjoy the fruits of their labor, for these are gifts from God." Don't live this life as a meaningless chase after the next best and biggest thing. You'll get to the end and feel empty. Stop and enjoy the gifts God has given you. Stop and remember to honor God—this will make life worth living.

Sometimes we think we should wait to experience some of the good things in life—wait until we have more money, wait until we have the job we want, wait until we have a mate. Consistently putting off enjoyment until later breeds discontentment. And later never really comes—because you're waiting for the "perfect" time and for everything to line up to begin to enjoy life. Tomorrow is just not promised—to any of us—young or old. I think the saddest thing would be to get to the end of this life and regret that you didn't do something or didn't try something. Live your life without regrets. Live your life like it's the only one you have. Yes, work hard, make plans, be wise and follow your heart; but at the end of the day (or throughout the day), don't forget to enjoy the life you have been given—today.

This life you have now was meant to be lived. Just do it—now.

Wisdom for the Journey

A person can do nothing better than to eat and drink and find satisfaction in their own toil. This too, I see, is from the hand of God, for without [God], who can eat or find enjoyment?... God gives wisdom, knowledge and happiness...

Ecclesiastes 2:24-26

14

Lessons on the Journey:
The Instinct to Learn
For Life

I KNOW YOU'VE GRADUATED AND COMPLETED A SECTION of this journey, but it is important to remember the value of lifelong learning. This is the type of learning that may not be captured in a textbook but more so by your eyes and hearts. The wise woman and prudent man knows that life itself is one big lesson. No day or no incident can pass you by without some sort of lesson—even if it's the reminder to cease the moment and enjoy what you have right now.

A bad moment in a day doesn't mean it's a lost day or even a bad day. It could be the day you learn an invaluable lesson. So the life-long learner is looking for the lesson, looking for the enjoyment, looking to cease it.

Failing or not making your target doesn't have to be bad—or the end; it can be feedback to help you succeed. Learning what you didn't know, learning how to do it differently, learning how to manage something else or new can all be lessons gleaned from falling on your face or being set back. Looking at each day and opportunity as a learning lesson takes intentionality and instinct. You need courage and perspective to learn all you can from every situation.

Research from observation can be quite conclusive; this explains why scientists have laboratories and not just libraries; why lawyers seek eyewitnesses at a crime scene; what we see often creates quite an impact. Are your eyes wide open to the lessons on this journey? Just as God used a safari in the country of South Africa to show me a new way to live and teach and run my businesses, your instinct can show you new things each and every day—whether you are on a safari or taking a trip to the supermarket. If your eyes and your heart and your mind are open, you can learn.

Regardless of what stage of life you find yourself in now, don't close your mind to learning. Shutting a book for a break is one thing, but closing your mind to new things, new thoughts, new ideas and concepts can be damaging. Who knows when the next ground-breaking idea will come to you? Where you will be? Who will help you see it? This is an exciting journey—so keep your head up and your eyes, ears and heart open. Something great is waiting to reveal itself to you.

As a lifelong learner on this journey, you can learn a few things, such as:

Your leadership style—by observing good and bad leaders as well as how others respond to you, you can figure out how best to inspire those who may work for you—in a business, on a committee, on a team, wherever. How do you inspire others? How can you sharpen those skills?

Your learning style—how do you best understand information—through reading, hearing, trying it out? The next time you have to learn something new, you can use your style to better grasp it. With today's multiple platforms in technology, there's no excuse not to really "get it." You can have it downloaded and listen to it over again, or read it on a computer, in a book, posted across a board. Or you can be more tactile and explore ways to learn it while touching, tasting, or doing something. The world is yours for the learning.

How do you manage your time? What a big question and what a critical one. Learning to get a handle on time can make a world of difference in your professional and personal life. No one can control every second of a minute of an hour, but you sure can put some perimeters around that hour and leave room to be flexible. Nothing breaks quicker than a stick that doesn't bend well. But, when you have realistically assessed how much time is needed for a task (and added some cushion), you can remain flexible and less stressed when the inevitable happens. Learn not to waste time or procrastinate; figure out what motivates you to get tasks done and repeat. Observe others, ask questions, try different techniques until you get some positive results (and then repeat).

Learn to control your emotions. We all have them, they make us human. But emotions shouldn't be what control us. You can feel. You need to feel. But feel your emotions, don't be controlled by them. An effective leader knows that she must keep her anger, sorrow and empathy in proper balance so she can focus on what is vital and important. Unchecked emotions can make us major in the minor and cause us to sweat the small stuff. Instinctive leaders don't have time for that. Learn how to handle emotions so you can think clearly and well under fire and pressure.

Another area of lifelong learning has to do with changing and adapting. You can't do new things with old tools. The world changes too quickly for that. Don't be afraid of new stuff. Go for it. Try it—over and over and over—until you get it. Hire the help you need, acquire the help you need—from whomever you have access to. And if you don't have access, gain it. Ask for it. Find it. There's nothing sadder than someone who can't grow because they are afraid to change. They are afraid of the new thing. There will be new things for the rest of your life. Learn to embrace them. And while your core and center and message won't change, your methods of doing things will need to change to keep up with the times and to be relevant and impactful. Don't become extinct because you don't want to bend your neck. Your survival and ability to succeed relies on your instinct, which can direct us to adapt to new terms.

The Apatosaurus, or brontosaurus, gives us an example of what can happen when we don't adapt. Scientists found that most dinosaurs became extinct because of predators and climate changes, but the Apatosaurus self-destructed for another reason. This dinosaur was very tall and was used to eating from the tallest trees. As the population of Apatosaurus grew, they ate all of the foliage from the top of the trees. They eventually died out because they couldn't get more food from the top of trees. However, had they only bent their necks a little bit, they would have found plenty of food. They were so used to eating from the radius they were accustomed to, they did not instinctively bend to look for food in new places.

Your instincts can point you to new things, new sources, new methods—you have to be flexible and in tune enough to know when to look. Resist self-destruction; be open to learning new things and new methods for life.

Time changes, leaders change, people change. God promises to be with us. We can use God's promise to Joshua as a promise to us (Joshua 1:5-6). "As I was with Moses, so I will be with you; I will never leave you nor forsake you. Be strong and courageous." The promises God made to give us a fulfilling life remain true to each generation. Following our instinct can guide us to the most fulfilling life imaginable—and then some.

Be strong and courageous. Life awaits.

Wisdom for the Journey

So now you can pick out what's true and fair,
find all the good trails!
Lady Wisdom will be your close friend,
and Brother Knowledge your pleasant companion.
Good Sense will scout ahead for danger,
Insight will keep an eye out for you.

Proverbs 2:9-11, MSG

15

Soar Eagle, Soar:
The Instinct to Fly

AS YOU PREPARE TO LAUNCH OUT AND GRASP your unlimited future, I want you to remember you've been called to soar like the eagle. Eagles are strong and uniquely set aside from other birds. An eagle's wing span can be 9 feet on each side. There's a certain height you have to be to interact with the eagle. It doesn't spend time on the ground with chickens. Eagles have vision and precision and they keep company only with eagles. They go where lesser birds can't fly and they do what lesser birds can't do.

Eagles make nests in high places—mountains, cliffs— so the eaglet is born high and understands even when it opens its eyes, that it is meant to live up high. Its vision is set high from birth. And when it is time to leave the nest, the bird has to spread its wings and soar. When nesting time is over, the bird needs to leave the comforts of the nest and learn to soar. The eagle stirs the nest and the younger bird has to move.

You've been prepared, you've been nurtured, you've

worked hard—now, it's time to move and soar. Spread your wings—watch them expand and take you to higher places. And remember the tools we've explored as you continue to tap into your instinct and soar.

Know who you are

Know what makes you unique. Know what you like and how you like it. And have the courage to enjoy it and to live your unique life. Your uniqueness points to your gifts and skills and what you were created specifically to do. Spend your life being you, not a replica of someone else. You were designed and created to be you and only when you live authentically can you be in tune with your instinct and unlock the treasure map of your life.

Develop your gifts

By investing in your innate gifts and skills, you are taking care of God's treasure. When your skills are ready and the timing is right, the best opportunities will show up and your instinct will recognize it. You will be prepared to launch ahead and work in your gifting area. Start now, wherever you are, truly using your gifts—to the best of your ability. Be honest. Sharpen when you need to sharpen. Look for opportunities to exercise your gifts and skills—and do it boldly and freely.

Connect to your source

It might sound like a cliché, but it is true: Jesus is your help. You don't exist in this world alone; you were created by a mighty and powerful God who has given us special help to walk this earth. Jesus was our example of man and God combined. He walked this earth reflecting God's nature, pointing to God's glory and plan for our lives. Jesus promised to send the comforter, God's spirit, to be with us on earth when he returned to heaven. You have God's spirit inside of you when you believe in Jesus. Tap into this amazing power today to know which way to go. God can provide guidance if you take the time to connect and recharge your batteries. You've got a lot to do out there, don't try to wing it with no power.

Make your job work for you

Know that a job is not always a career or a calling, but it can point toward one. The skills and gifts and relationships you develop at a job can launch you on a path toward an unlimited future. Do your best at each level on any job—no one should have to make you do your best. The flair you bring to even a mundane job can develop your gifts and skills and set you on a course to greater living and greater meaning.

Learn from your mentors

They can make this journey easier. They are walking tour guides who have already journeyed down a path you admire. Learn their lessons without needing to make all of their mistakes. Glean from them; give to them; look for them in every area of your life.

Travel with good friends

Who's riding with you? Are your friends helpful at this stage in your journey? Ride with people who can help you get to your destiny. Some friends are meant to be in our lives for a reason, a season, or a lifetime. Know the difference and act accordingly. Those who ride with us are a blessing, as they share our joys and sorrows and make life feel a bit sweeter. Invest in good and healthy friendships. Release the ones that have outgrown their season or who seem to travel on a path that doesn't point in the same direction as yours. Enjoy this journey with like-minded friends.

Make your home reflective of your journey

Your home is where you settle down for rest and relaxation and rejuvenation. These 3 Rs are critical to helping you live your best and to help you tap into your instinct. If your home environment is right, you can be more creative and focused. Do what you need to make your home a place that propels you toward your dreams; make sure the people you share your home with share your desire and ideals for this journey.

Live independently and interdependently

You have successfully moved from child to adult. Celebrate your rites of passage and refuse to dip back into the habits of a dependent. Make your own decisions. Live responsibly. Help those who raised you journey alongside you, not in front of you. It's time to say hello to adulthood—and all that comes with it. Create the boundaries you need to live by your instinct and reach for your destiny.

Love well

Finding love can be a journey in and of itself. Decide if you want to be in a lifelong relationship and if you are ready. Then put on your hunting gear, keeping all eyes open to find out what the interested person is all about. You want your future mate's heart and mind to be in line with yours. You want that person to support your goals and help you utilize your instinct, not distract from obtaining your purpose. Find someone you can love for who he or she is and who loves you exactly for who you are.

Cherish your true love as Christ cherishes the church, giving freely and sacrificially of your love. Make love happen and be prepared to make your love work.

Your money does matter

How do you handle your money? Instinct followers know how much they have and how much they have to spend. How's your budgeting skills? It is never too late to start living according to your budget. Find ways to increase your income and decrease your expenses if you have more month than money. You need money to tithe or donate to others and to save for retirement, emergencies and your special treats. The stress of money doesn't have to get in the way of your fulfilling your dreams. Learn to handle money well now; it's a trait that will take you well into your unlimited future—and it will pay off—in dollars and cents.

When it gets dark...

Despite what we grow up thinking, you shouldn't be afraid of the dark. There is value in the storm and dark nights. Your perspective is what makes the difference. When you encounter hard times—whether from life circumstances or some choices you've made—look up for help. Look for the message in the midst of the storm. What do you need to do differently next time? How do you need to learn to trust God, even in the midst of this situation. Keep journals or accounts of all of the rough times and long nights you've endured. You'll need to be reminded of how you overcame the next time it gets a little dark.

Serve others freely

Instinct followers go through life with their hands and eyes and hearts wide open. The fear of being hurt or being taken advantage of does not paralyze them or stop them from helping others. They gladly serve and give freely. It's the attitude of gratitude and the law of multiplication that serves them well. When you are grateful and recognize all of the gifts you've been given, you want to say thank you. There's no better way to show God you are grateful than to give to those who are hurting. Giving comes in many different forms and the instinct follower doesn't look at what he doesn't have. Instead she looks at what is needed and gives, just like the woman who gave two pennies. Miraculously, when we give—even when we feel deprived of energy, time, resources—we have enough. What we have multiples instead of decreases. Try living and giving freely today.

Lighten up and live

Achieving goals and reaching for your dreams is important, but remember life is meant to be enjoyed. You will get invigorated to work harder when you also take time to play and relax. Develop a habit of incorporating activities that you enjoy into your life regularly. Indulge yourself. Pamper yourself. Schedule vacations and stay-cations. Check off another bucket list item. You only live once—do it well and be fulfilled.

Learn for life

Each day presents a new opportunity to learn, another chance to discover something you didn't know—about life, yourself, work, this world. Welcome each day as a student awaiting a lesson. You will learn from experiences, information and people. Evolve and adapt while keeping your core beliefs in place. Your world and your mind will continue to open up wide and well.

Your unlimited future awaits.